New Mastermaths

Teacher's Book

4

Paul Briten

OXFORD

Great Clarendon Street, Oxford OX2 6DP

Oxford University Press is a department of the University of Oxford.

It furthers the University's objective of excellence in research, scholarship, and education by publishing worldwide in

Oxford   New York

Auckland   Cape Town   Dar es Salaam   Hong Kong   Karachi
Kuala Lumpur   Madrid   Melbourne   Mexico City   Nairobi
New Delhi   Shanghai   Taipei   Toronto

With offices in

Argentina   Austria   Brazil   Chile   Czech Republic   France   Greece
Guatemala   Hungary   Italy   Japan   Poland   Portugal   Singapore
South Korea   Switzerland   Thailand   Turkey   Ukraine   Vietnam

Oxford is a registered trade mark of Oxford University Press
in the UK and in certain other countries

British Library Cataloguing in Publication Data

Data available

ISBN 978-0-19-836116-9

10 9 8 7 6 5

Acknowledgments
Autumn Header Image © istockphoto (www.istockphoto.com)

Illustrated by IFA Design, Plymouth, UK
Cover illustration by Jonatronix
Page make-up by IFA Design, Plymouth UK
Printed in Great Britain by Ashford Colour Press, Gosport Hants

Paper used in the production of this book is a natural, recyclable product made from wood grown in sustainable forests. The manufacturing process conforms to the environmental regulations of the country of origin.

Contents

Introduction

The Mastermaths series

Mastermaths has been designed and written to provide motivating and differentiated practice for children aged 7 to 11. Based on the teaching order of the National Numeracy Strategy *Medium-Term Plans* for Year 3 and *Unit Plans* for Years 4 to 6, **Mastermaths** covers all the content and objectives outlined in the yearly teaching programmes detailed in the National Numeracy Strategy *Framework for Teaching Mathematics*.

Clearly this teaching order is only one possible route through the content. Objectives covered in each Unit of **Mastermaths** are made explicit in both the *Pupil Book* and the *Teacher's Book*. This ensures the greatest possible flexibility and ease of reference, enabling teachers to dip into the material as required. If you are following a different curriculum or teaching order, you may wish to match the **Mastermaths** Units to your own planning grids to create the teaching order most suitable for your own school's situation.

Mastermaths shares the assumption with the National Numeracy Strategy that successful maths lessons are built on high-quality direct and interactive teaching. Children should not be expected to teach themselves from textbooks and this is not how the **Mastermaths** series is intended to be used. Rather, it has been developed to support effective teaching by offering opportunities for consolidation, reinforcement and extension of practical work through carefully differentiated practice exercises. Above all, the pages have been designed to be engaging and exciting to make the learning of mathematics enjoyable for all children.

In the classroom

Whether you are following the *Unit Plans* or a different teaching order, **Mastermaths** is extremely easy to manage in the classroom. During the main teaching part of the lesson, you may wish to use pages or sections of **Mastermaths** in a variety of ways. For example:

- as a basis for teaching the whole class all working together on the same activities
- for discussion with groups of children to concentrate on particular objectives
- to develop problem-solving skills by using the 'Think about it…' activities for paired work
- as practice material for children to work on individually at an appropriate level
- as homework or assessment material to provide you with evidence of progress.

When planning your lessons or adapting the *Unit Plans* to meet the particular needs of your class, you will need to identify which pages or sections of **Mastermaths** you wish to use to provide children with the practice they need. The list of objectives for each page in the *Teacher's Book* and the clear learning outcomes identified at the base of each *Pupil Book* page will enable you to maintain the focus on the learning objectives throughout the lesson. Annotating your plans with notes showing how and when the material will be used with which children will help ensure that the pace of learning is maintained and that the needs of all children are taken into account.

Differentiation

Each Unit of **Mastermaths** covers all the objectives detailed in the corresponding National Numeracy Strategy *Unit Plan*. As recommended in the guidance for using them, it will be necessary to supplement the *Unit Plans* with additional activities to take account of the least and most able children. The breadth of differentiation offered by **Mastermaths** will help you support all the children in your class through graded practice designed to enhance learning.

Each Unit includes a lead-in section which revises objectives from the previous year level, and an extension activity which covers objectives from the next year level. The question numbers in these sections are colour coded to enable you to identify them quickly and easily (blue = Year 5 objective, purple = Year 6 objective, pink = Year 7 objective).

In addition, every page in each Unit of **Mastermaths** contains an open-ended challenge, to ensure that all children are given opportunities for enrichment and extension at a suitable level. These features will enable you to tailor lessons for groups or individuals and make certain that there is plenty of support material throughout the time you are teaching the Unit. Working at the correct level and having teacher support for the maximum amount of time possible, will develop children's confidence and assist their understanding and overall progress.

Assessment

The carefully differentiated questions in each Unit of **Mastermaths** will provide you with a starting point for assessing children's level of understanding. As well as using children's work to provide evidence of progress, dialogue between the teacher and children about their achievements and understanding will be necessary to ensure that assessment is a valuable exercise. Discussing the objectives that are written at the bottom of each *Pupil Book* page with the children will provide useful opportunities for assessment. These discussions will help inform future planning and the setting of individual targets.

Throughout **Mastermaths** there are many activities and investigations that encourage children to use and apply the mathematics they have learned. Often children are required to work with a partner in order to encourage development of mathematical language and key thinking skills. In particular, the 'Challenge' sections that appear on every page and the series of 'Think About It…' pages offer important formative assessment opportunities. By listening to the children and asking questions to probe children's learning, you will be able to judge whether key concepts and skills have been grasped.

Opportunities for more formal assessment are provided in the half-termly Review pages. These reviews provide sets of levelled questions for all the Units covered in the preceding half term and quickly alert the teacher to concepts that may be causing difficulties for individual children. In accordance with the National Numeracy Strategy expectations, work throughout **Mastermaths 4** corresponds to consolidation of level 4, and starting on level 5 for the mathematics attainment targets in the National Curriculum.

Pupil Book

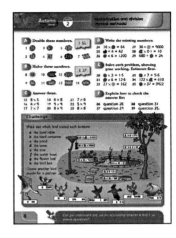

The bright and colourful *Pupil Book* pages have been developed to engage and motivate all children. They include the following features:

- a simple, consistent and easy-to-follow layout
- plenty of practice questions set out in carefully graded sections
- sample answers where appropriate to make questions completely clear and provide children with an indication of how to set out their answers
- challenges to encourage children to apply the skills they have learned
- clear learning outcomes for children to check their understanding.

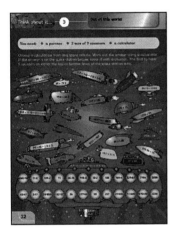

Interspersed throughout the **Mastermaths** Units there are a series of 'Think About It...' pages which revise the work of the preceding set of Units in an exciting, stimulating and often humorous setting. These practical games, challenges and activities provide enrichment and extension and are presented in a way that will capture children's interest and enthusiasm. Any equipment required (e.g. number cards, calculators, etc) is listed at the top of each page.

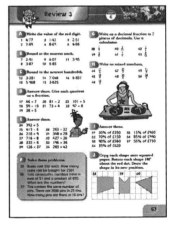

Each *Pupil Book* contains six Review pages arranged to slot into the half-termly Assess and Review units. The levelled assessment questions focus on checking children's understanding of the key objectives covered in the previous Units.

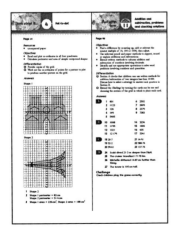

Teacher's Book

Detailed teaching notes for each page of the *Pupil Book* are provided from page 18 of this *Teacher's Book*. All objectives covered on the *Pupil Book* page are clearly listed. Each page also offers helpful guidance on differentiation, including references to the lead-in and extension questions, as well as further suggestions for other ways to support (U icon) or extend children (O icon).

Full answers are clearly presented for each page so that marking is made as simple as possible. Note that not all 'Think about it...' pages require answers as these are often open-ended games and practical activities.

Planning

The clear structure, carefully graded practice material and maximum flexibility of the **Mastermaths** series will enable you to easily incorporate the Units into your planning. The grids on the following pages will assist you with identifying how best to use the **Mastermaths** Units to support the scheme of work in your school. By referring to the Unit objectives you will quickly be able to reorder the Units if desired and adapt the teaching order to suit the needs of your class.

NNS Unit Plans

Mastermaths has been designed so that the content and teaching order link exactly with the National Numeracy Strategy *Unit Plans*. The termly grids on pages 8–10 summarise the objectives for each Unit for Year 6 and identify where this content is covered in the **Mastermaths 4** *Pupil Book* and *Teacher's Book*.

NNS Framework

If you have developed your own medium-term plans based on the NNS *Framework for Teaching Mathematics* for which the order of teaching differs from the *Unit Plans*, you may wish to use the grids on pages 11–14 to identify where particular topics or objectives are covered. These show at a glance how the **Mastermaths** Units relate to the strands and yearly teaching programmes of the *Framework* and will help you find relevant activities to support your own scheme of work.

Mathematics 5–14 for Scotland

Schools following the Mathematics 5–14 curriculum in Scotland will also find **Mastermaths** an excellent resource to support their teaching. **Mastermaths 4** is appropriate for Primary 7 pupils and covers work at levels D and E. The grids on pages 15–17 will show how **Mastermaths** maps onto the various strands and attainment targets to assist you with your planning. You may wish to dip in and out of Units when teaching different topics; these planning grids will help you identify where suitable activities may be found.

The National Curriculum in Wales

Mastermaths will also support teaching of the programme of study for mathematics set out in the National Curriculum in Wales. By using the grids on pages 11–14 and equating attainment targets for Number, Shape, Space and Measures, or Handling Data to the equivalent strands and objectives in the NNS *Framework*, you will be able to identify appropriate activities for your school's teaching order. Opportunities for Using and Applying Mathematics are embedded throughout the **Mastermaths** Units. **Mastermaths 4** is suitable for Year 6 pupils and comprises work corresponding to consolidation of level 4 and starting on level 5 attainment targets.

The Northern Ireland Curriculum

Schools in Northern Ireland will find the **Mastermaths** series useful in supporting the Programme of Study for Mathematics at Key Stage 2. The **Mastermaths** Units provide practice for work relating to the Attainment Targets for Number, Measures, Shape and Space, and Data Handling. Processes in Mathematics is embedded throughout as pupils are encouraged to use and apply mathematics. **Mastermaths 4** is suitable for Primary 7 pupils and covers work at levels 4 and 5. You may wish to use the termly grids on pages 8–10 to identify where specific objectives are covered, to help you integrate **Mastermaths** into your planning.

Autumn term			Mastermaths	
Unit	**Unit topic**	**Unit objectives**	**Pupil Book**	**Teacher's Book**
1	Place value	• **Multiply and divide decimals by 10 or 100 and integers by 1000, explain the effect.** • Identify and use appropriate operations (including combinations of operations) to solve problems involving numbers and quantities based on 'real life' or money, using one or more steps	5–7	18–19
2	Multiplication and division, mental methods	• Use the relationship between multiplication and division. • Use related facts and doubling and halving. • **Identify and use appropriate operations (including combinations of operations) to solve word problems.** • Approximate first.	8–10	19–20
3	Multiplication and division, mental methods	• Use pencil and paper methods to support, record or explain multiplications and divisions. • Extend written methods to short multiplication of numbers involving decimals. • Round up or down after division, depending on context. • **Identify and use the appropriate operations (including combinations of operations) to solve word problems involving numbers and quantities.** • Develop calculator skills and use a calculator effectively.	11–13	21–22
4	Fractions, decimals and percentages	• **Reduce a fraction to its simplest form by cancelling common factors.** • Recognize the equivalence between the decimal and fraction forms. • Use decimal notation for tenths and hundredths; extend to thousandths for measurements. • Know what each digit represents. • **Understand percentage as the number of parts in every 100.** • **Find simple percentages of small whole number quantities.**	15–17	23–24
5	Fractions, decimals, percentages, ratio and proportion	• **Round a number with two decimal places to the nearest tenth or to the nearest whole number.** • Recognize the equivalence between decimal and fractions, forms. • **Solve simple problems involving ratio and proportion.**	18–20	24–25
6a	Handling data	• Use the language associated with probability to discuss events, including those with equally likely outcomes. • **Solve a problem by representing, extracting and interpreting data in tables, graphs, charts** and diagrams, including those generated by a computer, for example; line graphs, bar charts with grouped discrete data. • Find the mode and range of a set of data. • Begin to find the median and mean of a set of data.	22–24	26–27
6b	Using a calculator	• Develop calculator skills and use a calculator effectively. • Check with the inverse operations when using a calculator. • Check with an equivalent calculation.	25–27	28–29
7	Assess and review		28	29
8	Shape and space: reasoning about shapes and measures	• Classify quadrilaterals using criteria such as parallel sides, equal angles, equal sides …. • Solve mathematical problems or puzzles, recognize and explain patterns and relationships (orally and in writing). • **Calculate perimeter of rectangles and area of simple compound shapes that can be split into rectangles.**	29–31	30–31
9	Measures	• Use, read and write standard metric units of length, km, m, cm, mm, including their abbreviations and relationships between them. • Convert smaller units to larger and vice versa: m to km, cm or mm to m. • Suggest suitable units and measuring equipment to estimate or measure length. • **Identify and use appropriate operations to solve word problems involving numbers and quantities (based on 'real life' or measures).** • Know rough equivalents of miles and kilometres. • Appreciate different times around the world.	33-35	32–33
10	Shape and space; position, movement and scales, solving problems	• **Read and plot co-ordinates in all four quadrants.** • Recognize where a shape will be after two translations. • **Identify and use appropriate operations (including combinations of operations) to solve word problems involving numbers and quantities** based on 'real life' or measures (including time), using one or more steps. • Choose and use appropriate number operations to solve problems and appropriate ways of calculating (mental, mental with jottings written methods, calculator). **Explain methods and reasoning.** • Record estimates and readings from scales to a suitable degree of accuracy. • Know imperial units, know rough equivalents of lb and kg, oz and g, miles and km, litres and pints or gallons.	36–38	33–34
11	Addition and subtraction, problems and checking solutions	• Find a difference by counting up; add or subtract the nearest multiple of 10, 100 or 1000, then adjust. • Use informal pencil and paper methods to support, record or explain additions and subtractions. • **Extend written methods to column addition and subtraction of numbers involving decimals.** • **Identify and use appropriate operations to solve word problems involving numbers and quantities.** • Check with the inverse operation when using a calculator.	40–42	35–36
12	Number sequences	• Solve mathematical problems or puzzles, recognize and explain patterns and relationships, generalize and predict. • Recognize and extend number sequences, such as the sequence of square numbers, or the sequence of triangular numbers. • Explain methods and reasoning, orally and in writing. • Develop from explaining a generalized relationship in words to expressing it in a formula using letters as symbols	43–45	37–38
13	Assess and review		46	38

Unit	Unit topic	Unit objectives	Pupil Book	Teacher's Book
1	Place value	• Find the difference between a positive and a negative integer, or two negative integers, in the context such as temperature or a number line, and order a set of positive and negative integers. • **Order a mixed set of numbers** or measurements with **up to 3 decimal places.** • Consolidate rounding an integer to the nearest 10, 100, or 1000. • Round a number with two decimal places to the nearest tenth or nearest whole number. • Develop calculator skills and use a calculator effectively.	47–49	39–40
2	Multiplication and division 1	• Use known facts and place value to consolidate mental multiplication and division. • Use the relationship between multiplication and division. • Express a quotient as a fraction, or as a decimal rounded to 1 decimal place. Dividing £ and p by a two-digit number to give £ and p. Round up or down after division depending on context. • Develop calculator skills and use a calculator effectively	50–52	40–41
3	Multiplication and division 2	• Understand and use the relationship between the four operations, and the principles (not the names) of the arithmetic laws. • Use brackets. • Use factors. • Use closely related facts. • **Extend written methods to: long multiplication of a three-digit by a two-digit integer**; short division of TU or HTU by U (mixed-number answer); division of HTU by TU (long division, whole-number answer); **short division of numbers involving decimals.**	53–55	42–43
4	Problem solving	• Choose and use appropriate number operations to solve problems, and appropriate ways of calculating: mental, mental with jottings, written methods, calculator. • Explain methods and reasoning. • Check with an equivalent calculation. • Develop calculator skills and use a calculator effectively.	57–59	44–45
5a	Fractions, decimals and percentages	• Order fractions by converting them to fractions with a common denominator, and position them on a number line. • **Use a fraction as an 'operator' to find fractions of numbers of quantities.** • Change a fraction to the equivalent mixed number. • Begin to convert a fraction to decimal using division. • Express simple fractions as percentages. • **Find simple percentages of small whole number quantities.** • Develop calculator skills and use a calculator effectively.	60–62	45–46
5b	Rotations and reflections	• Recognize where a shape will be after a rotation through 90° about one of its vertices. • Recognize where a shape will be after reflection: in a mirror line touching the shape at a point (sides of shape not necessarily parallel or perpendicular to the mirror line); in two mirror lines at right angles (sides of shape all parallel or perpendicular to mirror line).	64–66	47–48
6	Assess and review		67	49
7	Addition and subtraction	• Use known number facts and place value to consolidate mental addition/subtraction. • **Extend written methods to column addition and subtraction of numbers involving decimals.** • **Identify and use appropriate operations (including combinations of operations) to solve word problems involving numbers and quantities.** • **Explain methods and reasoning.** • Develop calculator skills and use a calculator effectively. • Check with the inverse operation when using a calculator. • Check the sum of several numbers by adding in reverse order. • Estimate by approximating then check result.	68–70	49–50
8	Angles, 2D and 3D shapes, perimeter and area	• Recognize and estimate angles. • **Use a protractor to measure and draw acute and obtuse angles to the nearest degree.** • Check that the sum of the angles in a triangle is 180 degrees. • Calculate angles in a triangle or around a point. • Describe and visualize properties of solid shapes such as parallel or perpendicular faces or edges. • Visualize 3D shapes from 2D drawings and identify different nets for a closed cube. • **Calculate the perimeter and area of simple compound shapes that can be split into rectangles.**	71–73	51–52
9	Measures and problem solving	• Use, read and write standard metric units (km, m, cm, mm, kg, g, l, cl, ml) of length, mass and capacity, including their abbreviations, and relationships between them. • Convert smaller to larger units (e.g. m to km, cm or mm to m, g to kg, ml to l) and vice versa. • Know rough equivalents of lb and kg, oz and g, miles and km, litres and pints or gallons. • **Identify and use appropriate operations (including combinations of operations) to solve word problems involving numbers and quantities** based on 'real life', money or measures, using one or more steps, and calculating percentages such as VAT. • Suggest suitable units to estimate or measure length, mass or capacity. • Suggest suitable measuring equipment. • Record estimates and readings from scales to a suitable degree of accuracy.	75–77	53–54
10	Ratio, proportion, data handling and problem solving	• **Solve simple problems involving ratio and proportion.** • **Solve a problem by** representing, **extracting and interpreting data in tables, graphs, charts** and diagrams, including those generated by a computer, for example: line graphs; frequency tables and bar charts with grouped discrete data.	78–80	54–55
11	Properties and reasoning about numbers	• Make general statements about odd or even numbers, including the outcome of products. • Know and apply simple tests of divisibility. Find simple common multiples. • Recognize prime numbers to at least 20. • Factorize numbers to 100 into prime factors. • Explain methods and reasoning, orally and in writing. • Solve mathematical problems or puzzles, recognize and explain patterns and relationships, generalize and predict. Suggest extensions asking 'What if …?' • Develop from explaining a generalized relationship in words to expressing it in a formula using letters as symbols (e.g. the cost of n articles at 15p each).	82-84	56–57
12	Assess and review		85	58

Unit	Unit topic	Unit objectives	Pupil Book	Teacher's Book
1	Decimals, fractions, percentages	• Multiply and divide decimals mentally by 10 or 100 and integers by 1000, and explain the effect. • Order a mixed set of numbers with up to three decimal places. • Consolidate rounding an integer to the nearest 10, 100 or 1000. • Round a number with two decimal places to the nearest tenth or whole number. • Reduce a fraction to its simplest form by cancelling common factors. • Use a fraction as an operator to find fractions of numbers or quantities. • Understand percentage as the number of parts in every 100. • Find simple percentages of small whole-number quantities.	86–88	58–59
2	Calculations	• Consolidate all (mental calculation) strategies from previous years. • **Extend written methods to column addition and subtraction of numbers involving decimals.** • **Derive quickly division facts corresponding to tables up to 10 x 10.** • **Extend written methods to:** **Short multiplication of numbers involving decimals.** **Long multiplication of a three-digit by a two-digit integer.** **Short division of numbers involving decimals.** • **Explain methods and reasoning.** • Use a calculator effectively. • Check results of calculations.	89–91	60–61
3	Shape and space	• **Read and plot co-ordinates in all four quadrants.** • **Use a protractor to measure and draw angles to nearest degree.** • **Calculate perimeter and area of simple compound shapes that can be split into rectangles.** • Classify quadrilaterals. • **Calculate angles in a triangle or around a point.** • Visualize 3-D shapes from 2-D drawing and identify different nets for a closed cube. • Recognize where a shape will be after reflection. • Recognize where a shape will be after two translations.	92-94	61–62
4	Problem solving 1	• Solve a problem by representing, extracting and interpreting data in tables, graphs, charts and diagrams, including those generated by a computer, e.g. line graphs, frequency tables and bar charts with grouped discrete data. • Find the mode and range of a set of data. Begin to find the median and mean of a set of data. • Use the language associated with probability to discuss events, including those with equally likely outcomes. • **Identify and use appropriate operations (including combinations of operations to solve word problems involving numbers and quantities) based on 'real life' or money, using one or more steps.** • **Explain methods and reasoning.**	96–98	63–64
5	Problem solving 2	• **Identify and use appropriate operations (including combinations of operations) to solve word problems involving numbers and quantities** based on 'real life'; money or measures (including time), using one or more steps, including converting pounds to foreign currency, or vice versa, and calculating percentages such as VAT. • **Explain methods and reasoning.** • **Solve simple problems involving ratio and proportion.** • Know rough equivalents of lb and kg, oz and g, miles and km, litres and pints or gallons. • Develop from explaining a generalized relationship in words to expressing it in a formula using letters as symbols, e.g. the cost of n articles at 15p. • Solve mathematical problems or puzzles, recognize and explain patterns and relationships, generalize and predict. Suggest extensions asking 'What if...?	99–101	65–66
6	Division, decimals, and problem solving	• **Derive quickly division facts corresponding to multiplication tables up to 10 × 10.** • **Order a mixed set of numbers with up to three decimal places.** • **Solve a problem by extracting and interpreting information presented in tables, graphs and charts.**	103–105	67–68
7	Perimeter, area, calculation and problem solving	• **Carry out column addition and subtraction of numbers involving decimals.** • **Calculate the perimeter and area of simple compound shapes that can be split into rectangles.** • **Identify and use the appropriate operations (including combinations of operations) to solve word problems involving numbers and quantities and explain methods and reasoning.**	106–108	68–69
8	Calculation, percentage, ratio and problem solving	• Multiply and divide decimals mentally by 10 or 100 and integers by 1000, and explain the effect. • Understand percentage as the number of parts in every 100 and find simple percentages of whole-number quantities. • Solve simple problems involving ratio and proportion.	109–111	70–71
9	Calculation, and problem solving	• **Carry out short multiplication and division of numbers involving decimals.** • **Carry out long multiplication of a three-digit by a two-digit integer.** • **Identify and use appropriate operations (including combinations of operations) to solve problems involving numbers and quantities, and explain methods and reasoning.** • Choose and use appropriate number operations to solve problems and appropriate ways of calculating: mental, mental with jottings, written methods, calculator. • Factorize numbers into prime factors. • Develop calculator skills and use a calculator effectively.	113–115	72–73
10	Fractions, proportion, ratio and problem solving	• **Reduce a fraction to its simplest form by cancelling common factors.** • **Use a fraction as an 'operator' to find fractions of numbers or quantities, e.g. $\frac{5}{8}$ of 32, $\frac{7}{10}$ of 40, $\frac{9}{100}$ of 400 centimetres.** • **Solve simple problems involving ratio and proportion.**	116–118	73–74
11	Angles, graphs and problem solving	• **Use a protractor to measure acute and obtuse angles to the nearest degree.** • **Read and plot co-ordinates in all four quadrants.** • **Solve a problem by extracting and interpreting information presented in tables, graphs and charts.**	120–122	75–76
12	**Assess and review**		123–124	77

NUMBERS AND THE NUMBERS SYSTEM

The table below maps curriculum objectives against teaching units grouped by term (Autumn, Spring, Summer).

Column groups:
- Autumn: 1, 2, 3, 4, 5, 6a, 6b, 7, 8, 9, 10, 11, 12, 13
- Spring: 1, 2, 3, 4, 5a, 5b, 6, 7, 8, 9, 10, 11, 12
- Summer: 1, 2, 3, 4, 5, 6, 7, 8, 9, 10, 11, 12

Place value, ordering and rounding

- **Multiply and divide decimals mentally by 10 or 100, and integers by 1000, and explain the effect.**
- Use the vocabulary of estimation and approximation.
- Consolidate rounding an integer to the nearest 10, 100 or 1000.
- Find the difference between a positive and a negative integer, or two negative integers, in a context such as temperature or the number line, and order a set of positive and negative integers.

Properties of numbers and number sequences

- Recognize and extend number sequences such as a sequence of square numbers, or a sequence of triangular numbers 1, 3, 6, 10, 15…
- Count on in steps of 0.1, 0.2, 0.25, 0.50… and then back.
- Make general statements about odd or even numbers, including the outcome of products.
- Recognize multiples up to 10 × 10. Know and apply simple tests of divisibility. Find simple common multiples.
- Recognize squares of numbers to at least 12 × 12.
- Recognize prime numbers to at least 20.
- Factorize numbers to 100 into prime factors.

Fractions, decimals and percentages, ratio and proportion

- Change a fraction such as $\frac{33}{8}$ to the equivalent mixed number $4\frac{1}{8}$, and vice versa.
- Recognize relationships between fractions: for example, that $\frac{1}{10}$ is ten times $\frac{1}{100}$ and $\frac{1}{16}$ is half of $\frac{1}{8}$.
- **Reduce a fraction to its simplest form by cancelling common factors in the numerator and denominator.**
- Order fractions such as $\frac{2}{3}$, $\frac{3}{4}$, and $\frac{5}{6}$ by converting them to fractions with a common denominator, and position them on a number line.
- **Use a fraction as an 'operator' to find fractions, including tenths and hundredths, of numbers or quantities (e.g. $\frac{5}{8}$ of 32, $\frac{7}{10}$ of 40, $\frac{9}{100}$ of 400 centimetres).**
- **Solve simple problems involving ratio and proportion.**
- Use decimal notation for tenths and hundredths in calculations, and tenths, hundredths and thousandths when recording measurements.
- Know what each digit represents in a number with up to three decimal places.
- Give a decimal fraction lying between two others (e.g. between 3.4 and 3.5).
- **Order a mixed set of numbers or measurements with up to three decimal places.**
- Round a number with two decimal places to the nearest tenth or the nearest whole number.
- Recognize the equivalence between the decimal and fraction forms of one half, one quarter, three quarters, one eighth … and tenths and hundredths and thousandths (e.g. $\frac{700}{1000} = \frac{70}{100} = \frac{7}{10} = 0.7$). Begin to convert a fraction to a decimal using division.
- **Understand percentage as the number of parts in every 100.** Express simple fractions such as one half, one quarter, three quarters, and tenths and hundredths, as percentages (e.g. know that $\frac{1}{3} = 33\frac{1}{3}\%$).
- **Find simple percentages of small whole-number quantities (e.g. find 10% of £500, then 20%, 40% and 80% by doubling).**

CALCULATIONS

CALCULATIONS	Autumn														Spring													Summer												
	1	2	3	4	5	6a	6b	7	8	9	10	11	12	13	1	2	3	4	5a	5b	6	7	8	9	10	11	12	1	2	3	4	5	6	7	8	9	10	11	12
Mental calculations strategies (+ and −)																																							
• Consolidate all strategies from previous year, including:																																							
find a difference by counting up;											•										•							•											
add or subtract the nearest multiple of 10, 100, or 1000, then adjust;											•										•							•											
use relationship between addition and subtraction;											•										•							•											
add several numbers.											•										•							•											
Use known number facts and place value to consolidate mental addition/subtraction (e.g. 470 + 380, 810 - 380, 7.4 + 9.8, 9.2 - 8.6).							•				•											•							•										
Pencil and paper procedures (+ and −)																																							
• Use informal pencil and paper methods to support, record or explain additions and subtractions.												•		•																									
Extend written methods to: column addition and subtraction of numbers involving decimals.												•		•							•																	•	
Understanding multiplication and division																																							
• Understand and use the relationships between the four operations, and the principles (not the names) of the arithmetic laws. Begin to use brackets.								•									•																						
• Express a quotient as a fraction, or as a decimal rounded to one decimal place. Divide £.p. by a two-digit number to give £.p. Round up or down after division, depending on the context.	•																										•												
Rapid recall of multiplication and division facts																																							
• Consolidate knowing by heart all multiplication facts up to 10 × 10.	•														•																	•	•			•			
• Derive quickly: squares of multiples of 10 to 100 (e.g. 60 × 60);	•														•																		•						
doubles of all two-digit numbers (e.g. 3.8 × 2, 0.76 × 2);	•														•																		•						
doubles of multiples of 10 to 1000 (e.g. 670 × 2);	•														•																		•						
doubles of multiples of 100 to 10 000 (e.g. 6500 × 2);	•														•																		•						
and the corresponding halves.	•														•																		•						
Mental calculation strategies (× and ÷)																																							
• Use related facts and doubling or halving. For example: double or halve the most significant digit first;	•														•																•		•		•			
to multiply by 25, multiply by 100 then divide by 4;	•															•																•							
double one number and halve the other;	•															•																•							
find the ×24 table facts by doubling the ×6 table;	•															•																•							
find sixths by halving thirds.	•															•																•							
• Use factors (e.g. 35 × 18 = 35 × 6 × 3).	•																•																						
• Use closely related facts (e.g. multiply by 49 or 51 by multiplying by 50 and adjusting; develop the ×17 table from the ×10 and ×7 table).	•																•														•		•		•			
• Partition (e.g. 87 × 6 = (80 × 6) + (7 × 6); 3.4 × 3 = (3 × 3) + (0.4 × 3)).	•																•														•		•		•			
• Use the relationship between multiplication and division.	•															•																•	•	•	•	•			
• Use known facts and place value to consolidate mental multiplication and division.	•															•																•	•	•	•	•			

	Autumn														Spring													Summer											
	1	2	3	4	5	6a	6b	7	8	9	10	11	12	13	1	2	3	4	5a	5b	6	7	8	9	10	11	12	1	2	3	4	5	6	7	8	9	10	11	12

CALCULATIONS

Pencil and paper procedures (× and ÷)

- Approximate first. Use informal pencil and paper methods to support, record or explain multiplications and divisions.

Extend written methods to:

- multiplication of ThHTU × U (short multiplication);
- short multiplication of numbers involving decimals;
- long multiplication of a three digit by a two-digit integer;
- short division of TU or HTU by U (mixed-number answer);
- division of HTU by TU (long division, whole-number answer);

Using a calculator

- Develop calculator skills and use a calculator effectively.

Checking results of calculations

- Check with the inverse operation when using a calculator.
- Check the sum of several numbers by adding in the reverse order.
- Check with an equivalent calculation
- Estimate by approximating (round to nearest 10 or 100 or 1000), then check result.
- Use knowledge of sums and differences of odd/even numbers.
- Use tests of divisibility.

SOLVING PROBLEMS

Making decisions

- Choose and use appropriate number operations to solve problems, and appropriate ways of calculating; mental, mental with jottings, written methods, calculator.

Reasoning and generalising about numbers or shapes

- Explain methods and reasoning, orally and in writing.
- Solve mathematical problems or puzzles, recognize and explain patterns and relationships, generalize and predict. Suggest asking 'What if...?'
- Make and investigate a general statement about familiar numbers or shapes by finding examples that satisfy it.

Develop from explaining a generalized relationship in words to expressing it in a formula using letters as symbols (e.g. the cost of n articles at 15p each).

Problems involving 'real life', money and measures

- **Identify and use appropriate operations (including combinations of operations) to solve word problems involving numbers and quantities** based on 'real life', money or measures (including time), using one or more steps, including converting pounds to foreign currency, or vice versa, and calculating percentages such as VAT.

Explain methods and reasoning.

HANDLING DATA

Handling data

- Use the language associated with probability to discuss events, including those with equally likely outcomes.
- **Solve a problem by representing, extracting and interpreting data in tables, graphs, charts and diagrams,** including those generated by a computer, for example: Line graphs (e.g. for distance/time, for a multiplication table, a conversi:on graph, a graph of pairs of numbers adding to 8);

Frequency tables and bar charts with grouped discrete data (e.g. test marks 0-5, 6-10, 11-15...).

- Find the mode and range of a set of data. Begin to find the median and mean of a set of data.

13

MEASURES, SHAPE AND SPACE

	Autumn														Spring													Summer											
	1	2	3	4	5	6a	6b	7	8	9	10	11	12	13	1	2	3	4	5a	5b	6	7	8	9	10	11	12	1	2	3	4	5	6	7	8	9	10	11	12
Measures																																							
• Use, read and write standard metric units (km, m, cm, mm, kg, g, l, ml, c l), including their abbreviations, and relationships between them. Convert smaller to larger units (e.g. m to km, mm to cm to m, g to kg, ml to l) and vice versa.								•		•													•				•		•										•
Know imperial units (mile, pint, gallon, lb, oz).										•																						•							
Know rough equivalents of lb and kg, oz and g, miles and km, litres and pints or gallons.										•	•													•															•
• Suggest suitable units and measuring equipment to estimate or measure length, mass or capacity.										•														•	•														
Record estimates and readings from scales to a suitable degree of accuracy.											•																												
• **Calculate the perimeter and area of simple compound shapes that can be split into rectangles.**									•					•									•			•							•						•
• Appreciate different times around the world.										•																	•												
Shape and space																																							
• Describe and visualize properties of solid shapes such as parallel or perpendicular faces or edges.																							•																
• Classify quadrilaterals, using criteria such as parallel sides, equal angles, equal sides…								•						•							•									•									
• Make shapes with increasing accuracy. Visualize 3-D shapes from 2-D drawings and identify different nets for closed cubes.																					•		•							•									
• Recognize where a shape will be after reflection : in a mirror line touching the shape at a point (sides of shape not necessarily parallel or perpendicular to the mirror line);																				•										•									
in two mirror lines at right angles (sides of shape all parallel or perpendicular to the mirror line).																			•	•																			
• Recognize where the shape will be after two translations.													•	•															•										
• **Read and plot co-ordinates in all four quadrants.**													•	•															•								•		
• Recognize and estimate angles.																							•															•	
Use a protractor to measure and draw acute and obtuse angles to the nearest degree.																							•				•		•								•	•	
Check that the sum of the angles of a triangle is 180° for example, by measuring or paper folding.																														•									
Calculate angles in a triangle or around a point.																					•								•	•									
Recognize where a shape will be after a rotation through 90° about one of its vertices.																				•																			•

Planning chart: columns are school weeks grouped by term (Autumn weeks 1–13, Spring weeks 1–12, Summer weeks 1–12). A bullet (•) marks the week(s) in which each target is addressed.

Strand	Level	Target	A1	A2	A3	A4	A5	A6a	A6b	A7	A8	A9	A10	A11	A12	A13	S1	S2	S3	S4	S5a	S5b	S6	S7	S8	S9	S10	S11	S12	Su1	Su2	Su3	Su4	Su5	Su6	Su7	Su8	Su9	Su10	Su11	Su12
Information handling																																								
Organize	D	By using diagrams or tables																																							
	D	By constructing graphs (bar, line, frequency polygon) and pie charts:																		•													•								
		- involving continuous data which has been grouped						•																									•								
Display	E	By constructing straight line and curved graphs for continuous data where there is a relationship such as direct proportion - travel, temperature, growth graphs											•																												
		By constructing pie charts of data expressed in percentages																																							
Interpret	D	From a range of displays and databases:																																							
		- by retrieving information subject to one condition						•																		•									•				•		
	E	By describing the main features of a graph so as to show an awareness of the significance of the information						•																										•		•					
	E	By calculating the average (mean) to compare sets of data								•																															•
Number, money and measurement																																								
Range and type of numbers	D	Work with: - whole numbers up to 100 000 (count, order, read/write)	•																																						
		- whole numbers up to a million (read/write only)	•																																						
		- fractions (all previous plus twentieths, fiftieths, hundredths) and equivalences among these and decimals (in applications)			•	•											•																								
		- percentages, decimals to 2 places and equivalences among these in applications in money and measurement			•	•									•	•																									
	E	Work with: - negative numbers (e.g. temperature)													•	•	•																								
		- all widely used fractions and equivalence among these and decimals (in applications)								•			•	•	•	•	•																							•	
		- decimals to 3 places (practical applications in measurement)						•	•	•			•	•												•															
Money	D	Use all UK coins/notes to £20 worth or more, including exchange	•																																						
	E	Use relationships between currencies to do simple calculations			•	•																																			
	D	Add and subtract:																																							
		- mentally for 2 digit whole numbers, beyond in some cases involving multiples of 10 or 100																												•											
		- without a calculator, for 4 digits with at most 2 decimal places (easy examples only)							•														•								•										
		- with a calculator, for 4 digits with at most 2 decimal places											•											•					•		•										
		- in applications in number, measurement and money								•			•											•	•						•		•							
Add and subtract	E	Add and subtract:																																							
		- mentally for 2 digit numbers including decimals								•			•				•														•										
		- without a calculator for 4 digits with at most 2 decimal places							•															•							•				•					
		- with a calculator for any number of digits with at most 3 decimal places																						•	•									•		•				
		- in applications in number, measurement and money																							•																
		- positive and negative numbers in applications such as rise in temperature													•																										
Multiply and divide	D	Multiply and divide:																																							
		- mentally for whole numbers by single digits (easy examples only)	•	•														•													•						•	•			
		- mentally for 4 digit numbers including decimals by 10 or 100	•																																		•	•			
		- without a calculator for 4 digits with at most 2 decimal places by a single digit			•																										•										
		- with a calculator for 4 digits with at most 2 decimal places by a whole number with 2 digits																				•									•							•			•
		- in applications in number, measurement and money	•																																						

Number, money and measurement

Strand	Level	Target	A1	A2	A3	A4	A5	A6a	A6b	A7	A8	A9	A10	A11	A12	A13	S1	S2	S3	S4	S5a	S5b	S6	S7	S8	S9	S10	S11	S12	Su1	Su2	Su3	Su4	Su5	Su6	Su7	Su8	Su9	Su10	Su11	Su12
			1	2	3	4	5	6a	6b	7	8	9	10	11	12	13	1	2	3	4	5a	5b	6	7	8	9	10	11	12	1	2	3	4	5	6	7	8	9	10	11	12
Multiply and divide	E	**Multiply and divide:**																																							
		- mentally for any numbers including decimals by 10, 100, 1000		•	•	•											•	•	•																					•	
		- without a calculator for 4 digits with at most 2 decimal places by a single digit			•	•												•																				•			
		- with a calculator for any pair of numbers but at most 3 decimal places in the answer			•														•																						•
		- in applications in number, measurement and money			•												•													•	•										
Round numbers	D	**Round any number** to the nearest appropriate whole number, ten or hundred				•																	•	•						•											
	E	**Round any number** to one decimal place					•																•	•						•	•										
	D	**Work with fractions and percentages:**																																							
		- find simple fractions ($\frac{1}{2}, \frac{3}{4}, \frac{1}{5}, \frac{60}{100}$) of quantities involving at most 4 digits (easy examples only)				•	•														•												•								
Fractions, percentages and ratio		**Work with fractions and percentages:**					•														•																				
		- mentally find widely-used fractions and percentages of whole-number quantities																			•																•	•			
	E	- with a calculator find a fraction or percentage of a quantity																			•									•							•	•			
		- without a calculator as previously defined																				•								•							•	•			
		Find ratios between quantities					•																				•										•	•	•		
		Find simple unitary ratio					•																				•	•										•	•		
Patterns and sequences	D	**Continue and describe more complex sequences**												•															•												
	E	**Continue and describe sequences:**																																							
		- involving square and triangular numbers												•												•															
		- find specified items in sequences												•												•															
		- prime numbers												•													•														
Functions and equations	E	**Use notation** to describe general relationships between 2 sets of numbers													•	•											•														
		Use and devise simple rules													•	•												•													
Measure and estimate		**Measure in standard units:**																																							
		- length: small lengths in millimetres; large lengths like buildings in metres									•	•											•	•						•											
		- weight: extended range of articles, for example own weight									•	•												•																	
		- volume: accuracy extended to small containers in millilitres; 1l = 1000ml										•													•																
	D	- area: right-angled triangles on cm-squared grids																								•															
		- temperature						•																						•											
		Recognize when kilometres are appropriate									•													•																	
		Select appropriate measuring devices and units for weight										•												•																	
		Be aware of common Imperial units in appropriate practical applications									•	•																					•								
		Estimate measurements:																																							
		- small lengths in millimetres									•	•																													
	E	- larger lengths in metres									•	•																													
		Read scales on measuring devices, including estimating between graduations									•	•																													
Time	E	**Work with time:**									•	•																					•	•							
		- use 24-hour times and equate with 12-hour times									•	•																					•	•							
		- calculate duration in hours/minutes, mentally if possible									•	•																					•	•							
		- time activities in seconds with a stopwatch									•	•																						•							

16

Table: Maths curriculum planning grid — Strand / Level / Target mapped across Autumn, Spring and Summer teaching weeks. (Dot placements are a best reading of the grid.)

Strand	Level	Target	A1	A2	A3	A4	A5	A6a	A6b	A7	A8	A9	A10	A11	A12	A13	Sp1	Sp2	Sp3	Sp4	Sp5a	Sp5b	Sp6	Sp7	Sp8	Sp9	Sp10	Sp11	Sp12	Su1	Su2	Su3	Su4	Su5	Su6	Su7	Su8	Su9	Su10	Su11	Su12
Number, money and measurement																																										
Perimeter, formulae, scales	D	Calculate perimeter of simple straight-sided shapes by adding lengths									•																		•							•	•				•
	E	Calculate using rules:																								•				•						•		•			•
		– areas of rectangles and squares																												•						•			•		•
Shape, position and movement																																										
Range of shapes	D	Collect, discuss, make and use 3D and 2D shapes:									•					•						•										•									
		– discuss 3D and 2D shapes referring to faces, edges, vertices, diagonals, sides, angles									•					•						•																			
		– identify and name equilateral and isosceles triangles				•																										•		•							
		– make 3D models, solid or skeletal, including using nets: cube and cuboid only																																•							
	E	Use properties of 2D and 3D shapes:									•	•																													
		– discuss the side, angle, diagonal properties cf quadrilaterals: square, rectangle, rhombus, parallelogram, kite, trapezium									•	•																													
		– define and classify quadrilaterals									•																														
Position and movement	D	Discuss position and movement:										•									•	•	•				•	•												
		– use a co-ordinate system to locate a point on a grid										•									•	•	•				•	•												
		– create patterns by rotating a shape																			•	•	•																		
	E	Discuss position and movement:									•	•									•	•					•					•								
		– use co-ordinates in all four quadrants to plot position									•	•									•	•					•					•								
Symmetry	D	Work with symmetry:									•	•																													
		– identify and draw lines of symmetry, generally up to 4									•	•																													
		– create symmetrical shapes									•																														
	E	Work with symmetry:																			•											•									
		– move a tile of a shape on a squared grid in order to translate, reflect or rotate the shape																			•												•								
Angle	D	Angles:																						•					•		•	•						•	•	
		– draw, copy and measure angles accurately within 5 degrees																						•					•		•	•						•	•	
	E	Angles:																						•																•	•
		– know that the sum of the angles in a triangle is two right angles																							•														•		•

17

Page 5

Objective
- Multiply and divide decimals by 10 or 100 and integers by 1000, explain the effect.

Differentiation

☹ Section A checks that children can multiply and divide any positive integer up to 10 000 by 10 or 100 and understand the effect. Section B checks that they can read and write whole numbers in figures and in words. Check that children know what each digit represents in the numbers in Section B.

Answers

A
1	640
2	4650
3	1320
4	56 270
5	49
6	327
7	62
8	69 510
9	95
10	49 650
11	519 600

B
12 three thousand, four hundred and ninety-six
13 fifty-three thousand, one hundred and twenty-five
14 sixty thousand, nine hundred and forty-two
15 five hundred and twelve thousand, six hundred and thirty-five
16 five hundred and sixty thousand and ninety-eight
17 one million, two hundred and thirty-four thousand, five hundred and sixty-seven
18 two million, nine hundred and forty-three thousand, six hundred and one
19 eight million, six hundred and forty-three thousand, two hundred and seventy-nine

C
20 Jack, Arthur, Fran
21 Max, Sarah, Sam
22 Joe
23 Anna, Carl, Ben, Sally

Challenge
Check children play the game correctly.

Page 6

Objective
- Multiply and divide decimals by 10 or 100 and integers by 1000, explain the effect.

Differentiation

🎧 Extend the work in Section A by working out how many pencils placed end to end would stretch across the room and around the perimeter of the room.

Answers

A
1 150 cm
2 15 000 cm
3 1·5 cm
4 Answers will vary.
5 Answers will vary.
6 Approximately 2 mm
7 100 g
8 1000 g (or 1 kg)
9 10 000 g (or 10 kg)
10 1 cm

B
11 *100 times*
12 100 times
13 1000 times
14 100 times
15 100 times
16 10 000 times

C
17 *1000 times*
18 1000 times
19 100 times
20 100 times

Challenge
a 46 × 100 = 4600
c 68 × 1000 = 68 000
d 0·37 × 1000 = 370
e 3·6 ÷ 10 = 0·36
f 3600 ÷ 1000 = 3·6
g 2·35 × 1000 = 2350
h 4720 ÷ 100 = 47·2
i 34·8 ÷ 100 = 0·348

Page 7

Objective
- Identify and use appropriate operations (including combinations of operations) to solve problems involving numbers and quantities based on 'real life' or money, using one or more steps.

Differentiation
- Check the answers for questions 1 to 4 using the inverse operation. Check answers to questions 5 and 6 using a calculator.
- Use a calculator to check answers for questions 7 to 11. Rewrite the clues in the *Challenge* so that Mia Money arrives at different banks.

Answers

 A

1	£11·00
2	£0·58 (58p)
3	58 notes
4	£58·90
5	£1500
6	£12·21
7	£5788·80
8	£10 700
9	€33·20
10	20 000 sweets
11	£288

Challenge
forty 50p coins = £20
£1·92 ÷ 3 = 64p
100 × £1·83 = £183
eighty 20p coins = £16
60 × £15 = £900
£16 400 ÷ 100 = £164
102 × 55p = £56·10
1001 × 99p = £990·99
Mia Money is visiting Invest Direct.

Page 8

Objectives
- Use the relationship between multiplication and division.
- Use related facts and doubling and halving.
- Approximate first.

Differentiation
- Section A and B check that children can use doubling and halving starting from known facts.
  Section C checks that they know multiplication facts by heart. Make the *Challenge* easier by creating a bird puzzle using only multiplication facts up to 10 × 10, including multiplication by 0 and 1.
- Write the inverse operation that can be used to check each answer for the questions in the *Challenge*.

Answers

A

1	52	4	174	7	1256
2	36	5	240		
3	122	6	430		

B

8	29	11	170	14	243
9	42	12	155		
10	80	13	280		

C

15	40	18	48	21	42
16	36	19	81	22	45
17	49	20	72	23	64

D

24	4	26	200	28	100
25	168	27	300	29	20

E

30	0·5	32	6	34	5
31	2·1	33	0·8	35	106

F

36	64 ÷ 16 = 4	38	20 × 24 = 480
37	9000 ÷ 30 = 300	39	5·6 ÷ 7 = 0·8

Challenge
a 20 × 500 = 10 000 jay
b 40 × 175 = 7000 goldfinch
c 0·6 × 30 = 18 sparrow
d 0·4 × 9 = 3·6 duck
e 2·2 × 8 = 17·6 crow
f 15 × 28 = 420 heron
g 200 × 23 = 4600 blackbird
h 300 × 0·3 = 90 robin

Page 9

Objective
● Use related facts and doubling and halving to multiply and divide.

Differentiation
◑ Check that children are using a doubling and halving method to answer questions in Section A. Discuss strategies for answering questions in Section B.
◓ Check answers to section A using the grid method. Extend the *Challenge* by asking for alternative methods for solving Zen's problems.

Answers

A
1	990
2	910
3	1085
4	800

5	1175
6	34
7	48

B
8	3080
9	3250
10	5760

11	36
12	40
13	5550

C

1 × 28 = 28	9 × 28 = 252
2 × 28 = 56	10 × 28 = 280
3 × 28 = 84	11 × 28 = 308
4 × 28 = 112	12 × 28 = 336
5 × 28 = 140	13 × 28 = 364
6 × 28 = 168	14 × 28 = 392
7 × 28 = 196	15 × 28 = 420
8 × 28 = 224	

D
14	448
15	560
16	700

17	1400
18	1764
19	3640

Challenge
46 × 25 = 1150

62 × 13 = 806

1600 ÷ 25 = 64

59 × 8 = 472

380 × 50 = 19 000

6500 ÷ 250 = 26

19 × 28 = 532

Children's methods will vary. Check they are appropriate.

Page 10

Objective
● Identify and use appropriate operations (including combinations of operations) to solve word problems.

Differentiation
◑ Discuss strategies for making sensible estimates for questions in Section A. Also check that children are able to extract the calculations from the problems.
◓ Ask children to set some 'Think of a number' problems for a partner similar to question 9. Only half of the possible answers are given on the rockets in the *Challenge*. Ask children to work out as many of the other possible answers as they can.

Answers

A
1	855 apples
2	£925
3	60 bags
4	672 counters
5	45 chairs
6	180 jars
7	100 bricks
8	59·4 cm
9	42·8
10	35 < 37 < 41, 24 ≤ 29 ≤ 29, 67 > 61 > 60
11	37 × 29 × 61 = 65 453

Challenge
Check children play the game correctly.

Page 11

Objective
- Use pencil and paper methods to support, record or explain multiplications and divisions.

Differentiation
◑ Sections A, B and C check that children can use written methods for short multiplication of HTU by U, long multiplication of TU by TU and short division of HTU by U. Check that they can give a sensible estimate for questions in Section D. For the *Challenge*, provide similar questions involving TU × U and HTU × U.

◐ Extend the *Challenge* by asking children to produce four incomplete grids for a partner. They should use the same size grids as in the *Challenge*, with missing numbers in the same places.

Answers

A
1	1308	**3**	2961	**5**	3864	**7**	1701
2	1155	**4**	3114	**6**	8658	**8**	6258

B
9	608	**11**	756	**13**	1665	**15**	1628
10	731	**12**	648	**14**	416		

C
16	108	**18**	62	**20**	65 r 5
17	85	**19**	70 r 1		

D
- **21** $4627 \times 4 = 16\,000 + 2400 + 80 + 28 = 18\,508$
- **22** $3697 \times 3 = 9000 + 1800 + 270 + 21 = 11\,091$
- **23** $5176 \times 5 = 25\,000 + 500 + 350 + 30 = 25\,880$
- **24** $4863 \times 7 = 28\,000 + 5600 + 420 + 21 = 34\,041$
- **25** $5862 \times 8 = 40\,000 + 6400 + 480 + 16 = 46\,896$
- **26** $46 \times 38 = 1200 + 180 + 320 + 48 = 1748$
- **27** $37 \times 26 = 600 + 140 + 180 + 42 = 962$
- **28** $54 \times 38 = 1500 + 120 + 400 + 32 = 2052$
- **29** $29 \times 35 = 600 + 270 + 100 + 45 = 1015$
- **30** $425 \times 24 = 8000 + 400 + 100 + 1600 + 80 + 20 = 10\,200$
- **31** $376 \times 32 = 9000 + 2100 + 180 + 600 + 140 + 12 = 12\,032$
- **32** $495 \times 28 = 8000 + 1800 + 100 + 3200 + 720 + 40 = 13\,860$
- **33** $625 \times 47 = 24\,000 + 800 + 200 + 4200 + 140 + 35 = 29\,375$

Challenge
a $8135 \times 4 = 32\,540$

×	8	1	3	5
4	32000	400	120	20

b $3974 \times 6 = 23\,844$

×	3	9	7	4
6	18000	5400	420	24

c $427 \times 35 = 14\,945$

×	4	2	7
3	12000	600	210
5	2000	100	35

d $962 \times 47 = 45\,214$

×	9	6	2
4	36000	2400	80
7	6300	420	14

Page 12

Objectives
- Use pencil and paper methods to support, record or explain multiplications and divisions.
- Extend written methods to short multiplication of numbers involving decimals.
- Develop calculator skills and use a calculator effectively.

Differentiation
◑ Work through the first one or two questions with the group before they start on Section C.

◐ Extend the work in Section C by using a chunking method for ThHTU ÷ U.

Answers

A
- **1** estimate 16, larger than actual answer, 15·36
- **2** estimate 15, larger than actual answer 13·7
- **3** estimate 24, larger than actual answer 22·38
- **4** estimate 12, larger than actual answer 11·56
- **5** estimate 35, smaller than actual answer 36·82
- **6** estimate 48, smaller than actual answer 48·56
- **7** estimate 54, larger than actual answer 51·21
- **8** estimate 16, smaller than actual answer 17·52
- **9** estimate 35, smaller than actual answer 36·3
- **10** estimate 54, larger than actual answer 52·02
- **11** estimate 27, smaller than actual answer 29·43

B
- **12** $6·09 \times 3 = 18·27$ or $2·03 \times 9 = 18·27$
- **13** $5·67 \times 6 = 34·02$
- **14** $3·78 \times 7 = 26·46$

C
15	29	**19**	47	**22**	24 r 11
16	26	**20**	38	**23**	42 r 13
17	47	**21**	26 r 8	**24**	28 r 15
18	23				

Challenge
$29 \times 18 = 522$
$3654 \times 6 = 21\,924$
$167 \times 23 = 3841$
$24 \times 26 = 624$
$792 \div 18 = 44$
$663 \div 13 = 51$
$7·14 \times 4 = 28·56$
$4·27 \times 6 = 25·62$
$2054 \times 3 = 6162$
$1493 \times 8 = 11\,944$

Total = 45 166·18
Calculator reads BIGGISH.

Page 13

Objectives
- Use pencil and paper methods to support, record or explain multiplications and divisions.
- Round up or down after division depending on context.
- Identify and use appropriate operations (including combinations of operations) to solve word problems involving numbers and quantities.

Differentiation
☹ Discuss estimates for Section A. Check that children are able to extract the calculation from the problems in Section B.

☺ Answer questions 8 to 13 without using a calculator. Check all answers in Section C using a calculator.

Answers

A
1 20 512
2 18 944
3 19
4 22

B
5 28
6 20
7 20

C
8 7
9 8
10 6
11 21·68
12 29·63
13 54·82
14 7·5
15 3
16 7·4
17 19·6

Challenge
Check children carry out the calculations correctly.

54·8 × 7·0 = 383·6	62·4 × 5·8 = 361·92
39 × 10·9 = 425·1	18·7 × 12·3 = 230·01
26·2 × 9·0 = 235·8	33·8 × 20·5 = 692·9
14·7 × 8·5 = 124·95	26·7 × 10·6 = 283·02
11·9 × 31·9 = 379·61	83·3 × 5·8 = 483·14

Page 14

Resources
- a dice
- two sets of 12 coloured counters
- a partner

Objectives
- Multiply and divide decimals by 10 or 100.
- Use the relationship between multiplication and division.
- Use related facts and doubling and halving.
- Use pencil and paper methods to support, record or explain multiplications and divisions.
- Extend written methods to short multiplication of numbers involving decimals.

Differentiation
☹ Use a calculator to check each answer.
☺ Work without a calculator.

Answers

Clockwise from Start:

4·85 × 5 = 24·25
4·6 × 10 × 10 = 460
4726 × 3 = 14 178
15 × 1010 = 15 150
36 × 29 = 1044
504 ÷ 8 = 63
double 527 = 1054
26 × 14 = 364
300 × 0·3 = 90
260 × 50 = 13 000
6300 ÷ 100 = 63
4600 ÷ 10 = 460
316 × 4 = 1264
1100 ÷ 25 = 44
5·36 × 7 = 37·52
25 × 16 = 400
1254 × 4 = 5016
547 × 5 = 2735
300 × 0·4 = 120
150 × 101 = 15 150
double 58 = 116
91 × 4 = 364
130 × 100 = 13 000
20 × 400 = 8000

Page 15

Objective
- Recognize the equivalence between the decimal and fraction forms.

Differentiation
- ↻ Section A checks that children can relate simple fractions including tenths and hundredths to their decimal representations. Section B checks that they can convert improper fractions to mixed numbers. Discuss strategies for ordering the fractions in Section C.
- ∩ Write another fraction equivalent to each of the fractions in Section F.

Answers

A
1	0·2	4	0·25	7	0·23	10	0·75
2	0·1	5	0·5	8	0·37	11	0·9
3	0·3	6	0·7	9	0·6	12	0·11

B
13	$2\frac{7}{10}$	16	$3\frac{1}{9}$	19	$5\frac{4}{5}$
14	$4\frac{1}{4}$	17	$12\frac{1}{3}$	20	$8\frac{6}{7}$
15	$3\frac{1}{5}$	18	$6\frac{8}{10}$	21	$8\frac{8}{9}$

C
22	$\frac{1}{4}$	25	$\frac{5}{6}$	28	$\frac{2}{9}$
23	$\frac{3}{4}$	26	$\frac{3}{4}$	29	$\frac{3}{10}$
24	$\frac{2}{3}$	27	$\frac{31}{100}$	30	$\frac{5}{12}$

D
31	$\frac{2}{10} = \frac{20}{100}$	34	$\frac{2}{5} = \frac{40}{100}$	36	$\frac{40}{100} = \frac{400}{1000}$
32	$\frac{4}{10} = \frac{40}{100}$	35	$\frac{1}{10} = \frac{100}{1000}$	37	$\frac{3}{5} = \frac{600}{1000}$
33	$\frac{3}{10} = \frac{30}{100}$				

E Answers will vary.
38	$\frac{2}{10}, \frac{3}{15}, \frac{5}{25}, \frac{20}{100}$	42 $\frac{10}{12}, \frac{15}{18}, \frac{20}{24}, \frac{25}{30}$
39	$\frac{2}{8}, \frac{3}{12}, \frac{4}{16}, \frac{5}{20}$	43 $\frac{6}{8}, \frac{9}{12}, \frac{12}{16}, \frac{15}{20}$
40	$\frac{2}{16}, \frac{3}{24}, \frac{4}{32}, \frac{5}{40}$	44 $\frac{18}{20}, \frac{27}{30}, \frac{36}{40}, \frac{45}{50}$
41	$\frac{6}{10}, \frac{9}{15}, \frac{12}{20}, \frac{15}{25}$	

F
45	$\frac{9}{15}$	47	$\frac{12}{15}$
46	$\frac{16}{24}$	48	$\frac{35}{50}$

Challenge
Answers will vary.

Page 16

Objectives
- Reduce a fraction to its simplest form by cancelling common factors.
- Recognize the equivalence between the decimal and fraction forms.
- Use decimal notation for tenths and hundredths.
- Know what each digit represents.

Differentiation
- ↻ Check that the children know what each digit represents in the decimal fractions in Section E.
- ∩ Extend the *Challenge* by asking children to devise a set of similar clues to send another message.

Answers

A
1	$\frac{4}{5}$	7	$\frac{4}{5}$	12	$\frac{5}{8}$
2	$\frac{2}{5}$	8	$\frac{3}{10}$	13	$\frac{1}{3}$
3	$\frac{1}{4}$	9	$\frac{1}{3}$	14	$\frac{8}{25}$
4	$\frac{3}{4}$	10	$\frac{1}{3}$	15	$\frac{2}{25}$
5	$\frac{2}{3}$	11	$\frac{2}{5}$	16	$\frac{11}{125}$
6	$\frac{1}{5}$				

B
17	$\frac{1}{4}, \frac{3}{10}, \frac{11}{20}, \frac{3}{5}$	20	$\frac{200}{1000}, \frac{1}{4}, \frac{3}{10}, \frac{2}{5}$
18	$\frac{3}{20}, \frac{1}{5}, \frac{1}{4}, \frac{3}{10}$	21	$\frac{2}{5}, \frac{1}{2}, \frac{11}{20}, \frac{600}{1000}$
19	$\frac{3}{5}, \frac{7}{10}, \frac{3}{4}, \frac{16}{20}$	

C
22	b	26	f	30	n
23	h	27	c	31	o
24	d	28	j	32	m
25	e	29	k	33	l

D
34	0·3	38	0·29
35	0·7	39	0·021
36	0·9	40	0·013
37	0·16	41	0·028

E
42	$\frac{3}{100}$	46	$\frac{99}{100}$
43	$\frac{7}{100}$	47	$\frac{1}{100}$
44	$\frac{9}{100}$	48	$\frac{37}{100}$
45	$\frac{1}{4}$	49	$\frac{83}{100}$

Challenge
The message reads:

Urgent all agents prepare for action now!

Page 17

Objectives
- Use decimal notation for tenths and hundredths; extend to thousandths for measurements.
- Understand percentage as the number of parts in every 100.
- Find simple percentages of small whole number quantities.

Differentiation
- ☋ For the Challenge remove the cards with fractions in twentieths and the equivalent percentage cards.
- ☊ Discuss what each digit represents in a number with three decimal places.

Answers

A
1	370 cm	4	225 cm
2	420 cm	5	127 cm
3	180 cm	6	865 cm

B
7	4·3 kg	10	2·36 kg
8	2·5 kg	11	1·472 kg
9	2·2 kg	12	8·692 kg

C
13 $\frac{7}{10} = \frac{70}{100} = 70\%$ 16 $\frac{2}{5} = \frac{40}{100} = 40\%$
14 $\frac{4}{10} = \frac{40}{100} = 40\%$ 17 $\frac{3}{20} = \frac{15}{100} = 15\%$
15 $\frac{8}{10} = \frac{80}{100} = 80\%$ 18 $\frac{9}{10} = \frac{90}{100} = 90\%$

D
19	£125	22	£33
20	60 centimetres	23	630 kilometres
21	9 litres	24	£33

E
25	1·42 m	29	764 ml
26	0·015 kg	30	91 sweets
27	873 m	31	153 boys
28	1740 mm		

Challenge
Pairs as follows:
5% = $\frac{1}{20}$, 10% = $\frac{1}{10}$, 15% = $\frac{3}{20}$, 20% = $\frac{1}{5}$, 25% = $\frac{1}{4}$,
30% = $\frac{3}{10}$, 35% = $\frac{7}{20}$, 40% = $\frac{4}{10}$, 45% = $\frac{9}{20}$, 50% = $\frac{1}{2}$,
55% = $\frac{11}{20}$, 60% = $\frac{3}{5}$, 65% = $\frac{13}{20}$, 70% = $\frac{7}{10}$, 75% = $\frac{3}{4}$,
80% = $\frac{4}{5}$, 85% = $\frac{17}{20}$, 90% = $\frac{9}{10}$, 95% = $\frac{19}{20}$, 100% = 1

Page 18

Objective
- Round a number with two decimal places to the nearest tenth or the nearest whole number.

Differentiation
- ☋ Sections A and B check that the children can round a whole number to the nearest 10 or 100. Section C checks that they can round a number with one or two decimal places to the nearest integer. Check that children use the correct strategies to find the complements in Sections D, E, F and G.
- ☊ Extend the *Challenge* by asking children to write a different set of numbers with two decimal places for the telephones so that Crocko Dial talks to another character.

Answers

A
1	30	3	30	5	20
2	80	4	50	6	80

B
7	300	9	300	11	300
8	500	10	200	12	1000

C
13	5	18	10	22	8
14	6	19	2	23	7
15	2	20	3	24	5
16	7	21	6	25	6
17	7				

D
26	62	28	59	30	88
27	74	29	13	31	26

E
32	0·8	34	0·65	36	0·71
33	0·25	35	0·37	37	0·57

F
38	400	40	850	42	350
39	750	41	150	43	50

G
44	£8·50	46	£10·15	48	£6·73
45	£7·80	47	£15·31	49	£11·11

H
50	3·7 m			52	8·4 m
51	5·3 m			53	14·8 m

Challenge
43·79 rounds to 43·8
60·19 rounds to 60·2
56·64 rounds to 56·6
19·91 rounds to 19·9
46·85 rounds to 46·9
27·38 rounds to 27·4
10·11 rounds to 10·1
Crocko Dial is talking to Al Sation.

Objectives
- Recognize the equivalence between decimals and fractions.
- Develop calculator skills and use a calculator effectively.

Differentiation
☻ Work with the children on the first three questions in Section A. Some may need support in rounding decimals to two decimal places.
☻ Extend the *Challenge* by asking children to work out the smallest and largest fractions in Section A.

Answers

A

1	0·14	8	0·59
2	0·13	9	0·26
3	0·17	10	0·22
4	0·29	11	0·63
5	0·27	12	0·21
6	0·55	13	0·58
7	0·21		

B

14	0·29, 0·33, 0·13	$\frac{1}{8}, \frac{2}{7}, \frac{1}{3}$
15	0·38, 0·313, 0·308	$\frac{4}{13}, \frac{5}{16}, \frac{3}{8}$
16	0·08, 0·10, 0·22	$\frac{1}{12}, \frac{2}{21}, \frac{5}{23}$
17	0·8, 0·82, 0·46	$\frac{6}{13}, \frac{4}{5}, \frac{9}{11}$
18	0·49, 0·38, 0·42	$\frac{3}{8}, \frac{5}{12}, \frac{49}{100}$
19	0·86, 0·82, 0·94	$\frac{9}{11}, \frac{6}{7}, \frac{15}{16}$
20	0·09, 0·10, 0·16	$\frac{1}{11}, \frac{2}{21}, \frac{3}{19}$

C

21	0·249	23	0·151
22	0·23	24	0·16

D 25–30 Answers will vary.

Challenge
$\frac{1}{3} = 0·33$

$\frac{7}{20} = 0·35$

$\frac{1}{7} = 0·14$

$\frac{1}{5} = 0·20$

$\frac{2}{15} = 0·13$

$\frac{7}{45} = 0·16$

$\frac{100}{650} = 0·15$

$\frac{9}{50} = 0·18$

$\frac{5}{30} = 0·17$

$\frac{5}{24} = 0·21$

a $\frac{3}{11}$

b $\frac{7}{20}$

c 0·13

Objective
- Solve simple problems involving ratio and proportion.

Differentiation
☻ Check that the children understand the language of ratio and proportion.
☻ Change the number to be multiplied in Section D.

Answers

A

1 2 yellow squares to every green square
2 7 yellow squares to every 5 green squares
3 3 yellow squares to every 2 green squares
4 8 yellow squares to every 3 green squares.

B

5 1 in every 3 is yellow
6 7 in every 12 are yellow
7 3 in every 5 are yellow
8 8 in every 11 are yellow.

C

9 18 boys
10 60 children
11 1 in every 4 children are in red house
12 7 in every 10 sheep
13 £288

D

14	5·556	16	38·889
15	5·278	17	18·556

Challenge
a Numbers to 2 decimal places:

	= 100	= 1000	= 245	= 79	= 1110
17 ×	5·88	58·82	14·41	4·65	6·47
19 ×	5·26	52·63	12·89	4·16	5·79
37 ×	2·70	27·03	6·62	2·14	2·97
23 ×	4·35	43·48	10·65	3·43	4·78
13 ×	7·69	76·92	18·85	6·08	8·46

b Numbers to 3 decimal places:

	= 100	= 1000	= 245	= 79	= 1110
17 ×	5·882	58·824	14·412	4·647	6·471
19 ×	5·263	52·632	12·895	4·158	5·789
37 ×	2·703	27·027	6·622	2·135	2·973
23 ×	4·348	43·478	10·652	3·435	4·783
13 ×	7·692	76·923	18·846	6·077	8·462

Page 21

Resources
- cm-squared paper
- scissors

Objectives
- Reduce a fraction to its simplest form by cancelling common factors.
- Recognize the equivalence between the decimal and fraction forms.
- Use decimal notation for tenths and hundredths.
- Know what each digit represents.

Differentiation
- ☺ Provide a photocopy of the grid on cm-squared paper. Ask children to cross off answers on the grid before cutting.
- ☻ Produce some different clues to give the same answers.

Answers

1	$\frac{3}{10}$
2	$\frac{1}{5}$
3	$\frac{2}{15}$
4	$\frac{8}{15}$
5	$\frac{3}{5}$
6	$\frac{2}{3}$
7	$\frac{5}{8}$
8	$\frac{7}{20}$
9	0·125
10	0·55
11	0·45
12	375
13	190

0·45	$\frac{2}{5}$	0·85	0·1	0·4	375	$\frac{13}{15}$
0·375	$\frac{3}{20}$	$\frac{14}{15}$	0·95	$\frac{3}{5}$	$\frac{1}{5}$	290
$\frac{1}{4}$	$\frac{1}{3}$	0·5	$\frac{3}{5}$	90	$\frac{1}{15}$	0·15
$\frac{5}{8}$	$\frac{2}{15}$	275	0·125	$\frac{4}{15}$	$\frac{2}{3}$	$\frac{4}{5}$
$\frac{7}{10}$	$\frac{7}{15}$	$\frac{1}{2}$	0·9	0·65	0·55	0·75
0·7	190	390	0·625	110	$\frac{1}{10}$	$\frac{3}{10}$
0·875	0·25	$\frac{8}{15}$	$\frac{3}{4}$	$\frac{9}{10}$	$\frac{11}{15}$	$\frac{7}{20}$

The spy has entered the country, he is about to leave the airport, stop him quickly.

Page 22

Objectives
- Use the language associated with probability to discuss events, including those with equally likely outcomes.
- Solve a problem by representing, extracting and interpreting data in tables, graphs and charts, including those generated by computer, for example: bar charts with grouped discrete data.

Differentiation
- ☺ Section A revises previous work on probability. Check that the children have a strategy for organizing the data before they complete the bar chart for the *Challenge*.
- ☻ Extend the *Challenge* by asking children to draw another bar chart to represent the information, using different intervals, e.g. 0-29, 30-59, etc. Ask them to write five questions about the new bar chart for a partner.

Answers

A
1. poor chance
2. even chance
3. answers will vary
4. answers will vary
5. even chance
6. good chance.

B
7. yellow or grey
8. yellow, blue or purple

C
9. $\frac{1}{6}$
10. $\frac{1}{4}$
11. $\frac{1}{2}$
12. $\frac{4}{10}$ or $\frac{2}{5}$

Challenge

a

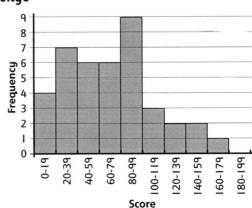

b Answers will vary.

Objectives
- Solve a problem by representing, extracting and interpreting data in tables, graphs and charts, including those generated by computer.
- Find the mode and range of a set of data.
- Begin to find the median and mean of a set of data.

Differentiation
◑ Check that the children are able to interpret pie charts before undertaking the work in Sections A and B.

Answers

A
1 $\frac{1}{2}$	3 $\frac{1}{4}$
2 $\frac{1}{8}$	4 $\frac{1}{8}$

B
5 6	7 3
6 3	8 12

C
9 18	11 3
10 9	12 6

D
13 range £31, mode £23, mean £28, median £26

14 range £26, mode £48, mean £50, median £48

15 range £20, mode £199, mean £199, median £199

16 range £5·89, mode £0·64, mean £3·20, median £3·67

Challenge
Check children play the game correctly.

Objectives
- Solve a problem by representing, extracting and interpreting data in tables, graphs and charts, including those generated by computer, for example line graphs.
- Find the mode and range of a set of data.
- Begin to find the median and mean of a set of data.

Differentiation
◑ For the *Challenge*, work out the range of times and the median time.
◖ Interpret information from other conversion graphs (e.g. grams/ounces). Ask children to construct a conversion graph (e.g. pounds/Euros; °C/°F), then write questions about the graphs for a partner.

Answers

A
1   5 °C
2   7 °C
3   7 °C
4   10 °C
5   mean 6 °C, median 5 °C, range 12 °C

B
6   16 km
7   40 km
8   72 km
9   64 km
10   48 km
11   20 km
12   50 miles
13   31 miles
14   12·5 miles
15   28 miles
16   40 miles
17   19 miles

C
18   70
19   63·5
20   93
21   67
22   144
23   73

Challenge
Check children play the game correctly.

Page 25

Objectives
- Develop calculator skills and use a calculator effectively.
- Check with the inverse operations when using a calculator.

Differentiation
⊎ Work in pairs for the *Challenge* and discuss findings in a group. Give the correct answer for each mistake.

ᴖ Extend the *Challenge* by asking children to set a similar challenge for a partner.

Answers

A
1. wrong, correct answer is 4448
2. correct
3. wrong, correct answer is 8796
4. wrong, correct answer is 10 695
5. correct
6. wrong, correct answer is 1169·94
7. wrong, correct answer is 30·43
8. wrong, correct answer is 3693·1
9. correct

B

Question		Estimate	Answer	Check (inverse operation)
	623 × 14	8000	8722	8722 ÷ 14 = 623
10	365 × 98·4	40 000	35 916	35 916 ÷ 365 = 98·4
11	463 × 152	100 000	70 376	70 376 ÷ 152 = 463
12	8811 ÷ 33	300	267	267 × 33 = 8811
13	42 × 1·67	80	70·14	70·14 ÷ 1·67 = 42
14	9021 − 6892	2000	2129	2129 + 6892 = 9021
15	427 + 1698 + 248	2300	2373	2373 − 427 − 248 = 1698
16	0·95 × 6	6	5·7	5·7 ÷ 6 = 0·95
17	261·8 − 7·35	250	254·45	254·45 + 7·35 = 261·8
18	491·38 − 196·7	300	294·68	294·68 + 196·7 = 491·38

Challenge
a. 13·4 − 6·8 = 6·6 (subtracted 6 from 13, then 0·4 from 0·8)
b. correct
c. 1008 × 12 = 12 096 (divided instead of multiplying)
d. correct
e. 126·9 + 34·68 = 161·58 (added decimal places wrongly)
f. ⁻26 + 47 = 21 (forgot negative number)
g. correct
h. 12·8 × 11·5 = 147·2 (forgot decimal point)

Page 26

Objective
- Develop calculator skills and use a calculator effectively.

Differentiation
⊎ Check that the children can use brackets. Work through one or two questions with the group before they work on Section D. It may be beneficial for children to work in pairs for Sections D and E.

ᴖ Extend the *Challenge* by giving different answers for each of the calculations.

Answers

A
1. 14 + (7 × 4) = 42
2. 16 × (7 + 3) = 160
3. (12 × 9) − 3 = 105
4. (9 + 6) × 4 = 60
5. 14 − (6 × 2) = 2
6. 16 + (24 × 2) = 64
7. 11 × (5 + 6) = 121

B
8–14 Answers will vary.

C
15–21 Answers will vary.

D
22. 2077
23. 725
24. 918
25. 1148
26. 4
27. 1524
28. 3588
29. 424
30. 215·3

E
31. (25 + 11) ÷ (100 ÷ 25) = 9
32. (324 − 225) − (6 × 11) = 33
33. (14 × 9) + (500 × 2) = 1126
34. (24 × 4) − (18 × 4) = 24
35. (25 + 24) ÷ (21 ÷ 3) = 7
36. (247 ÷ 13) + (156 + 89) = 264

Challenge
Check children play the game correctly.

Page 27

Objective
- Develop calculator skills and use a calculator effectively.

Differentiation
- Check that the children have understood Section C before moving on to Section D. Work in pairs for the *Challenge*. The last part of the *Challenge* could be a group activity.
- Extend the *Challenge* by asking children to find four consecutive numbers that when multiplied together give the answers 32 760, 255 024, 982 080.

Answers

A
1	12×13	4	38×39	7	19×20
2	24×25	5	56×57	8	96×97
3	28×29	6	48×49	9	101×102

B
	Numbers	Product
10	31 32	992
11	32 33	1056
12	33 34	1122
13	34 35	1190
14	35 36	1260
15	36 37	1332
16	37 38	1406
17	38 39	1482
18	39 40	1560

C
19	64	21	68	23	72
20	66	22	70	24	74

D
25	80	28	100	31	210
26	82	29	142	32	444
27	84	30	136	33	1998

Challenge
a The number is 1.
11111111 ÷ 9 = 1234567·8
b 11 × 12 × 13 = 1716
c 24 × 25 × 26 = 15 600
d 30 × 31 × 32 = 29 760
e *Rules*
- Start with a 3-digit number.
- Multiply the hundreds digit by 2
- Add 1
- Multiply by 5
- Add the tens digit
- Multiply by 2
- Add 1
- Multiply by 5
- Add the units digit
- Subtract 55
- You end up with the number you started with

The puzzle works for all 3-digit numbers.

Page 28

Answers

A
1	80	5	60
2	680	6	600
3	72	7	70
4	390	8	280

B
9	1058	21	11·8
10	1025	22	40·81
11	1152	23	31·52
12	38	24	15·84
13	672	25	51·45
14	2856	26	15·84
15	21 185	27	48
16	25 774	28	36
17	7674	29	58
18	66 472	30	46
19	16 584	31	41
20	16 533	32	28

C
33	$\frac{4}{5}$	38	$\frac{3}{25}$
34	$\frac{16}{25}$	39	$\frac{1}{9}$
35	$\frac{5}{16}$	40	$\frac{1}{25}$
36	$\frac{2}{3}$	41	$\frac{1}{20}$
37	$\frac{2}{5}$		

D
42	0·430 m	45	0·636 m
43	0·382 m	46	0·281 m
44	0·509 m	47	0·999 m

E
48	350	51	140
49	30	52	415
50	225	53	104

F
54	0·9	57	0·37
55	0·3	58	0·141
56	0·18		

G
59	range 20, mode 38, median 38, mean 37
60	range 23, mode 85, median 86, mean 87

H
61	1715	64	18 144
62	2046	65	47
63	2652		

Page 29

Objectives
- Classify quadrilaterals using criteria such as parallel sides, equal angles, equal sides.
- Solve mathematical problems or puzzles, recognize and explain patterns and relationships (orally and in writing).

Differentiation
↻ Sections A and B check that children have understood previous work on classifying shapes according to their properties.

∩ List all the shapes they know that fit the criteria in each of the *Challenge* questions.

Answers

A   Check that the following shapes have been drawn correctly:
1. a square
2. any quadrilateral with 2 right angles
3. a rhombus
4. a rectangle
5. rectangle or parallelogram
6. square, rhombus or kite

B

Quadrilateral		
Colour	Could be	Could not be
Red	*Rectangle*	12 Kite
	7 Trapezium	13 Rhombus
Yellow	8 Parallelogram	14 Square
	9 Rhombus	15 Rectangle
Blue	10 Rectangle	16 Kite
	11 Square	17 Rhombus

C   **18–22** Check shapes have been drawn correctly.

D   Two of the following properties for each shape.
23. 4 equal sides, 2 opposite pairs of parallel sides, 2 lines of symmetry, no right angles
24. one pair of parallel sides, four straight sides
25. 2 pairs adjacent sides equal, diagonals cross at right angles, 1 line of symmetry, one pair of opposite angles equal
26. opposite sides parallel, opposite angles equal

Challenge
Check children play the game correctly.

Page 30

Objectives
- Classify quadrilaterals using criteria such as parallel sides, equal angles, equal sides.
- Calculate perimeter of rectangles and simple compound shapes that can be split into rectangles.

Differentiation
↻ In the *Challenge* discuss how the lengths of unmarked sides can be calculated.

∩ On cm-squared paper, draw three 'complicated' shapes each having a perimeter of 36 cm.

Answers

A   1

	has 4 right angles	does not have 4 right angles
has 4 equal sides	square	rhombus
does not have 4 equal sides	rectangle	trapezium, kite

B
2. kite
3. rhombus
4. isosceles trapezium

C
5. 11·5 cm
6. 15·5 cm
7. 31·5 cm
8. 14·5 cm

Challenge
a. 70 m
b. 52 m
c. 44 m
d. 80 m

Page 31

Objectives
- Solve mathematical problems or puzzles, recognize and explain patterns and relationships (orally and in writing).
- Calculate perimeter of rectangles and area of simple compound shapes that can be split into rectangles.

Differentiation
↻ Check that children remember the formula for the area of a rectangle.

⌒ Discuss strategies for working out the dimensions of the outside of the path in question 19. Extend the work in Section E by changing the dimensions/shape of the lawn and the costs of the slabs and grass seed.

Answers

A

1	$6\,cm^2$	3	$6\,cm^2$	5	$6\,cm^2$
2	$6\,cm^2$	4	$6\,cm^2$	6	$6\,cm^2$

B

7	12 cm	9	12 cm	11	14 cm
8	14 cm	10	12 cm	12	10 cm

C
13 Answers will vary.
14 Answers will vary.

D
15 20 cm (if limited to integer values of lengths)
16 12 cm

E
17 56 m
18 32 m
19 48 m
20 Grass seed costs £28·80, paving costs £160, total cost is £188·80.

Challenge

Page 32

Resources
- a calculator
- two sets of 9 counters
- a partner

Objective
- Develop calculator skills and use a calculator effectively.

Differentiation
↻ Work with a partner using 10 counters. Place all ten counters and score a point for each counter placed on the top row. Try to beat the record.

⌒ Use two sets of 12 counters. The first player to place all twelve counters wins the game.

Answers

$2647 + 8978 = 11\,625$
$374·64 ÷ 14 = 26·76$
$749·64 ÷ 12 = 62·47$
$1908 ÷ 18 = 106$
$65 × 1·68 = 109·2$
$342·9 − 13·83 = 329·07$
$13·7 × 11·9 = 163·03$
$463·94 − 186·3 = 277·64$
$0·68 × 15 = 10·2$
$99·8 × 60·2 = 6007·96$
$(37 + 84) ÷ (132 ÷ 12) = 11$
$16 × 175·5 = 2808$
$225 × 226 = 50\,850$
$(96 × 8) − (73 × 7) = 257$
$47 × 48 = 2256$
$8·7 ÷ 0·15 = 58$
$1296 ÷ 54 = 24$
$(6·8 × 11·5) − (11·1 × 6) = 11·6$
$746 × 29 = 21\,634$
$8751 − 987 = 7764$
$36 × 25·3 = 910·8$
$149·73 ÷ 69 = 2·17$
$(17 × 3·6) + (18 × 2·4) = 104·4$
$29·84 × 16·5 = 492·36$

Page 33

Objectives
- Use, read and write standard metric units of length, km, m, cm and mm, including their abbreviations and relationships between them.
- Convert smaller units to larger and vice versa: m to km, cm or mm to m.
- Suggest suitable units and measuring equipment to estimate or measure length.

Differentiation
- Section A revises previous work on the relationships between standard metric units of length. Remind children how to measure accurately using a ruler.
- Extend the *Challenge* by working out the new snailometer reading if: Skiddy crawled the length of the table; Sloppy crawled across the room. (Measure to the nearest centimetre.)

Answers

A
1	4500 m	4	3920 m	7	9630 m
2	4900 m	5	6120 m	8	10470 m
3	6750 m	6	4680 m		

B
9	2·128 km	11	0·063 km	13	0·220 km
10	3·604 km	12	7·628 km		

C
14	4270 m	17	7 m	20	4030 m
15	3906 m	18	302 m	21	6500 m
16	17659 m	19	3206 m		

D
22	65 mm	24	100 mm
23	76 mm	25	43 mm

E
26	6·5 cm	28	0·1 m
27	0·043 m	29	0·075 m

F
30	464 m, 464·3 m	33	418 m, 417·6 m
31	270 m, 270·5 m	34	185 m, 185·1 m
32	265 m, 265·0 m		

Challenge
Answers will vary.

Page 34

Objectives
- Use, read and write standard metric units of length, km, m, cm and mm, including their abbreviations and relationships between them.
- Convert smaller units to larger and vice versa: m to km, cm or mm to m.
- Suggest suitable units and measuring equipment to estimate or measure length.
- Know rough equivalents of miles and kilometres.

Differentiation
- For Section A provide a grid with the axes drawn and scales added.
- Give distances to local towns in miles. Work out each distance as accurately as possible in km.

Answers

A Answers will vary.

B
1	38 km
2	26 km
3	48 km
4	42 km
5	19 km
6	28 km

C
7	31 miles
8	16 miles
9	8 miles
10	18 miles
11	33 miles
12	38 miles

D 13–16 Answers will vary.

Challenge
Check children play the game and measure correctly.

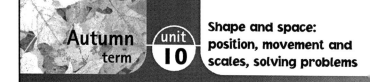

Page 35

Objective
* Appreciate different times around the world.

Differentiation
 Revise 24-hour clock times.

Extend Section A by working out the times in the different countries when you are: getting up, having lunch, finishing school, going to bed.

Answers

A

1   1:00 p.m.
2   3:00 a.m.
3   6:00 a.m.
4   12 midnight
5   4:00 p.m.
6   11:00 a.m.
7   10:00 p.m. (previous day)
8   5:00 a.m.

B

9   25 minutes   12   02:50 the next day
10   100 minutes   13   8525 km
11   16:50   14   4 hours

Challenge
a   4:00 a.m. the next day   c   2:00 p.m.
b   2:00 a.m.   d   10:00 a.m.

Page 36

Objectives
* Read and plot co-ordinates in all four quadrants.
* Recognize where a shape will be after two translations.

Differentiation
 Section A checks that children can read and plot points in the first quadrant. For questions 5 to 8 check that the points have been plotted correctly before they are joined with straight lines. Provide photocopies of co-ordinate grids for Section D.

Extend the *Challenge* as follows: each player has 10 counters. The first player generates ten points on the grid by using the two packs of cards as before and places a counter at each point. If a point is repeated place both counters at that point. The second player now places ten counters in the same way. Score 1 point for every counter in the first quadrant, 2 for the second quadrant, and so on. The player with the most points wins the game.

Answers

A

1   parallelogram   5   right-angled isosceles
2   square   triangle
3   isosceles triangle   6   kite
4   trapezium   7   rectangle
                           8   hexagon

B   9-12   Answers will vary.

C   13

14   square a: (2,¯3)
     (1,¯2) (0,¯3) (1,¯4)
     square b: (2,¯3)
     (1 ¯2) (2,¯1) (3,¯2)
     square c: (2,¯3)
     (1,¯3) (1,¯2) (2,¯2)

D

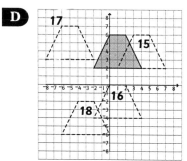

Challenge
Check children play the game correctly.

33

Page 37

Objectives
- Identify and use appropriate operations (including combinations of operations) to solve word problems involving numbers and quantities based on 'real life' or measures (including time) using one or more steps.
- Choose and use appropriate number operations to solve problems and appropriate ways of calculating (mental, mental with jottings, written methods, calculator). Explain methods and reasoning
- Know imperial units; know rough equivalents of lb and kg.

Differentiation
◑ Check that the children can extract the calculations from the problems. For the *Challenge* provide a grid with the axes drawn and scales added. Choose suitable objects for weighing.

◔ Find the mass of different children in pounds and kilograms.

Answers

A
1 3·65 m of fabric is left.
2 Ashley is 2·225 km behind Seb.
3 Stu can take another 4·2 kg.
4 The path will stretch 7·048 m (12 slabs + 11 gaps).
5 29 470 seats
6 126 300 seats
7 1 540 860 seats
8 35 lengths of plastic can be cut.
9 John's journey takes 87 minutes (1 hour 27 minutes).
10 Anish has run 9 times further than Abi.

Challenge

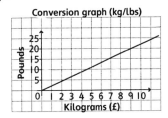

Conversion graph (kg/lbs)

apples 19 lbs
mushrooms 1 lb
carrots 5·5 lbs
bananas 9·5 lbs
potatoes 21 lbs
charcoal 26·5 lbs

Page 38

Objectives
- Record estimates and readings from scales to a suitable degree of accuracy.
- Know imperial units, know rough equivalents of litres and gallons, inches and centimetres, pounds and kilograms, pints and litres.

Differentiation
◑ Section F should be supplemented with practical activities. Work in pairs for the *Challenge*.

◔ Work in pairs to find: an object that weighs approximately one pound; a length that is approximately one yard; an object that is approximately one foot/one inch long; a container that holds approximately $\frac{1}{2}$ pint of water.

Answers

A
1 14 l
2 11 l
3 36 l

B
4 18 pints
5 32 pints
6 71 pints

C
7 25 cm
8 45 cm
9 75 cm
10 210 cm
11 158 cm

D
12 8 inches
13 14 inches
14 40 inches
15 24 inches

E
16-21 Answers will vary.

F
22 12·5 kg, 16 kg
23 6·7 kg, 7·75 kg
24 8·83 kg, 9·25 kg
25 9·37 kg, 9·7 kg

G
26-29 Answers will vary.

Challenge
a–d Answers will vary.
e 1 pint ≈ 571 ml

Page 39

Resources
- cm-squared paper

Objectives
- Read and plot co-ordinates in all four quadrants.
- Calculate perimeter and area of simple compound shapes

Differentiation
⊖ Provide copies of the grid.
⊕ Work out the co-ordinates of points for a partner to plot to produce another picture on the grid.

Answers

Shape 1

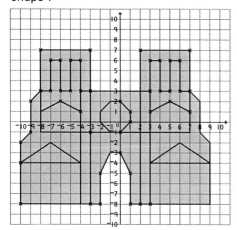

Shape 2

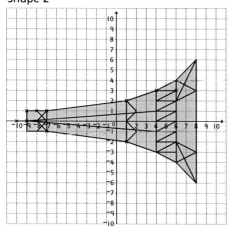

1 Shape 2
2 Shape 1 perimeter = 82 cm
   Shape 2 perimeter = 51·4 cm
3 Shape 1 area = 226 cm², Shape 2 area = 188 cm²

Page 40

Objectives
- Find a difference by counting up; add or subtract the nearest multiple of 10, 100 or 1000, then adjust.
- Use informal pencil and paper methods to support, record or explain additions and subtractions.
- Extend written methods to column addition and subtraction of numbers involving decimals.
- Identify and use appropriate operations to solve word problems involving numbers and quantities.

Differentiation
⊖ Section A checks that children can use written methods for addition/subtraction of two integers less than 10 000. Discuss how to select a strategy to answer each question in Section B.
⊕ Extend the *Challenge* by turning the cards one by one and choosing the section of the grid in which to place each card.

Answers

A
1	601	6	2502
2	1123	7	2609
3	126	8	2379
4	149	9	7383
5	5405		

B
10	1008	14	3234
11	1199	15	1606
12	1321	16	435
13	12179	17	5341

C
18	20·7	21	14·91
19	52·2	22	588·76
20	59·61	23	137·76

D
24 Scubi dived 21·3 m deeper than Dipti.
25 The cruiser travelled 171·95 km.
26 Michelle slithered 14·87 cm further than Slimy.
27 The tower is 105 cm tall.

Challenge
Check children play the game correctly.

Page 41

Page 41

Objectives
- Use informal pencil and paper methods to support, record or explain additions and subtractions.
- Extend written methods to column addition and subtraction of numbers involving decimals.
- Identify and use appropriate operations to solve word problems involving numbers and quantities.
- Check calculations using inverse operations.

Differentiation
- Use a calculator to check answers for Sections A and B. Work in pairs for Section C.
- Explain how the answers for section C were checked. Extend the *Challenge* by changing the fares and/or zone charges.

Answers

A 1–8 Answers will vary.

B 9–16 Answers will vary.

C
- 17 £30·05
- 18 £10·05
- 19 £106·95
- 20 £289·80
- 21 £147·10
- 22 £123·75
- 23 £250·05 (9 paying passengers)
- 24 In a car longer than 4 m.
- 25 5 children

Challenge
- a £4·70
- b £5·20
- c £13·60
- d 4
- e Answers will vary.

Page 42

Page 42

Objective
- Check with the inverse operation when using a calculator.

Differentiation
- Discuss strategies for the *Challenge* that would lead to a better chance of matching one of the answers. The first player to place five counters on the grid wins.
- For the *Challenge* take another turn each time you place a counter. The first player with 10 counters on the grid wins.

Answers

A
- 1 *answer must end in a 0*
- 2 answer must end in 5
- 3 answer must be less than 3000
- 4 answer must 8
- 5 answer must end in 00
- 6 answer must end in 2
- 7 answer must be less than 188

B
- 8 26
- 9 29·9
- 10 21·5
- 11 11·25
- 12 15·5

C
- 13 $28·44 \div 4·5 \approx 6·32$ *answer is wrong*
- 14 $1·92 \times 5 = 9·6$ answer is correct
- 15 $9·2 \div 2·5 = 3·68$ answer is wrong
- 16 $880·01 \div 65 = 13·54$ answer is correct
- 17 $1263·71 + 259·67 = 1523·38$ answer is wrong
- 18 $9402·85 - 996·48 = 8406·37$ answer is correct

D Estimates may vary. Suitable estimates might be:
- 19 100, accurate answer will be smaller
- 20 4, accurate answer will be smaller
- 21 700, accurate answer will be larger
- 22 12, accurate answer will be smaller
- 23 16, accurate answer will be smaller
- 24 80, accurate answer will be smaller
- 25 1440, accurate answer will be smaller
- 26 320, accurate answer will be larger

Challenge
Check children play the game correctly.

Page 43

Objective
- Recognize and extend number sequences formed by counting on or back in steps of different size, extending beyond zero when counting back.

Differentiation
◑ Sections A, B and C revise previous work on sequences. Work through one or two examples before the children start the *Challenge*.

◐ Extend the *Challenge* by working out the fifteenth term for the score in each sequence.

Answers

A
1. 27, 33, 39
2. 27, 38
3. 39, 31
4. 0, ⁻7
5. ⁻4, 4

B
6. 40, 47, 54   add 7 each time
7. 28, 36, 44   add 8 each time
8. 23, 14, 5   subtract 9 each time
9. 62, 74, 86   add 12 each time
10. 8, 13, 21   each term is sum of previous 2 terms

C
11. 82
12. ⁻31
13. 134
14. 89

D
15. 7·0, 7·2, 7·4, 7·6, 7·8   add 0·2 each time
16. 2·0, 2·25, 2·5, 2·75   add 0·25 each time
17. 7·75, 7·25, 6·75, 6·25   subtract 0·5 each time
18. 0·5, 0·25, 0, ⁻0·25   subtract 0·25 each time
19. 9·8, 9·5, 9·2, 8·9   subtract 0·3 each time
20. 0·1, ⁻0·3, ⁻0·7, ⁻1·1   subtract 0·4 each time

E
21. 46
22. 66
23. 82
24. 77
25. 33

Challenge
Check children play the game correctly.

Page 44

Objectives
- Recognize and extend number sequences, such as the sequence of square numbers or the sequence of triangular numbers.
- Solve mathematical problems or puzzles, recognize and explain patterns and relationships, generalize and predict.
- Develop from explaining a generalized relationship in words to expressing it in a formula using letters as symbols.

Differentiation
◑ Work with the group on Sections C and D and on the *Challenge*.

Answers

A
1. 19
2. 28
3. 100
4. 361

B
5.

Number of term	1	2	3	4	5	6	7	8	9	10
Squares	1	2	3	4	5	6	7	8	9	10
Circles	4	6	8	10	12	14	16	18	20	22

6.

Number of term	1	2	3	4	5	6	7	8	9	10
Triangles	1	2	3	4	5	6	7	8	9	10
Circles	3	5	7	9	11	13	15	17	19	21

C
7. 62
8. 100
9. $2n + 2$
10. number of circles $= 2n + 2$

D
11. 20
12. 401
13. $2n + 1$
14. number of circles $= 2n + 1$

Challenge
a. $2n$
b. $4n - 3$
c. $3n + 1$
d. n^2

Page 45

Objectives
- Solve mathematical problems or puzzles, recognize and explain patterns and relationships, generalize and predict.
- Develop from explaining a generalized relationship in words to expressing it in a formula using letters as symbols.

Differentiation

 In section A, children find the first ten terms and the twentieth term for each sequence.

 In a group of 5 people, everyone shakes hands with everyone else. How many handshakes is that? How many handshakes when there are a group of 10 people? 20 people?

Answers

A 1

Number of term	1	2	3	4	5	6	10	50	100
Number of counters	3	5	7	9	11	13	21	101	201

Rule: Start at 3. Add 2 to each number.

2

Number of term	1	2	3	4	5	6	10	50	100
Number of counters	2	5	8	11	14	17	29	149	299

Rule: Start at 2. Add 3 to each number.

3

Number of term	1	2	3	4	5	6	10	200	1000
Number of counters	5	7	9	11	13	15	23	403	2003

Rule: Start at 5. Add 2 to each number.

B
4 $2n + 1$
5 $3n - 1$
6 $2n + 3$

C
7 26
8 77
9 1502

D
10 43
11 248
12 498

E
13 60
14 389
15 781

F
16 3
17 10
18 28
19 45
20 105
21 190

Challenge
a 10
b 15
c 45
d 105

Page 46

Answers

A
1 42 cm
2 44 cm
3 74 m

B
4 5360 m
5 4980 m
6 3060 m
7 4900 m
8 3750 m
9 10 070 m
10 100 030 m

C
11 6·327 km
12 4·031 km
13 2·000 km
14 4·006 km
15 0·495 km
16 6·940 km
17 0·202 km

D
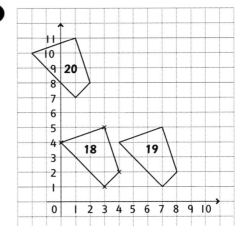

E
21 28·8
22 105·3
23 70·5
24 14·71
25 586·3

F
26 $16 \times 9·25 = 148$
27 $66·2 - 27·5 = 38·7$
28 $0·08 \times 54 = 4·32$
29 $4·75 + 37·85 = 42·6$
30 $4·76 \times 18·5 = 88·06$
31 $43·68 \div 8 = 5·46$

G
32 7·0, 7·7, 8·4, 9·1, 9·8   add 0·7 each time
33 3·25, 2·75, 2·25, 1·75, 1·25   subtract 0·5 each time
34 0·4, 0, ‾0·4, ‾0·8, ‾1·2   subtract 0·4 each time
35 49·5, 40·5, 31·5, 22·5, 13·5   subtract 9 each time

H
36 $2n + 2$
37 $2n + 1$
38 $2n$

Page 47

Objectives

- Find the difference between a positive and a negative integer, or two negative integers, in a context such as temperature or a number line, and order a set of positive and negative integers.
- Round a number with two decimal places to the nearest whole number.
- Develop calculator skills and use a calculator effectively.

Differentiation

◖ Section A checks that children can order a set of numbers with the same number of decimal places. Section B checks that they can round a number with one or two decimal places to the nearest integer. Section C checks that they can order a set of positive and negative integers in the context of temperature. Check that children can use the 'sign change' key on the calculator before working on Section E.

◖ Write a calculation that gives the answer ‾23, ‾35, etc.

Answers

A
1	3·12, 3·21, 3·27, 3·71, 3·72
2	4·45, 4·57, 4·75, 5·47, 7·54
3	5·01, 5·11, 5·19, 5·91, 5·99
4	6·02, 6·12, 6·21, 6·22, 6·26
5	6·18, 6·66, 6·68, 8·16, 11·68

B
6	4	10	12
7	6	11	12
8	9	12	7
9	5		

C
13	‾7 °C, ‾2 °C, 0 °C, 6 °C, 8 °C
14	‾11 °C, ‾5 °C, ‾4 °C, 1 °C, 6 °C
15	‾20 °C, ‾16 °C, ‾12 °C, ‾4 °C, 0 °C
16	‾12 °C, ‾10 °C, ‾8 °C, ‾7 °C, 2 °C
17	‾8 °C, ‾5 °C, 4 °C, 7 °C, 9 °C

D
18	‾7 °C	21	‾9 °C
19	‾3 °C	22	‾15 °C
20	4 °C		

E
23	‾2	28	‾8
24	3	29	‾15
25	10	30	‾21
26	13	31	22
27	2	32	‾44

Challenge
Check children play the game correctly.

Page 48

Objectives

- Find the difference between a positive and a negative integer, or two negative integers.
- Order a mixed set of numbers or measurements with up to three decimal places.

Differentiation

◖ For the *Challenge* give tortoise distances in metres to two decimal places and have only two sections on a grid for tenths and hundredths of a metre.

◖ The *Challenge* introduces the addition of numbers with three decimal places.

Answers

A

Mr Sven Dallot			
Date	Money out	Money in	Balance
1st Jan			£130
2nd Jan	£142		‾£12
1 3rd Jan		£50	£38
2 4th Jan	£37		£1
3 7th Jan	£260		‾£259
4 8th Jan	£140	£20	‾£379
5 9th Jan		£500	£121
6 10th Jan	£371·50		‾£250·50

B
7	$\frac{4}{100}$	11	$\frac{7}{100}$
8	$\frac{7}{10}$	12	$\frac{6}{10}$
9	$\frac{8}{100}$	13	$\frac{2}{10}$
10	$\frac{3}{10}$		

C
14	2·36 m, 3·02 m, 3·06 m, 3·26 m, 3·62 m
15	4·59 m, 4·95 m, 4·99 m, 5·01 m, 5·11 m
16	10·01 m, 10·1 m, 10·11 m, 11·01 m, 11·1 m

D
17	$\frac{4}{100} = \frac{40}{1000}$	20	$\frac{8}{100} = \frac{80}{1000}$
18	$\frac{9}{100} = \frac{90}{1000}$	21	$\frac{20}{100} = \frac{200}{1000}$
19	$\frac{10}{100} = \frac{100}{1000}$		

E
22	0·139	25	0·023
23	0·406	26	0·120
24	0·037		

Challenge
Check children play the game correctly.

Page 49

Objectives
- Round a number with two decimal places to the nearest tenth or nearest whole number.
- Order a mixed set of numbers or measurements with up to three decimal places.

Differentiation
- Check that the children are able to round any integer up to 10 000 to the nearest 10, 100 or 1000.
- Measure five lengths in the classroom and record them as metres to the nearest: 0·01 m; 0·001 m.

Answers

A
1	0·126, 0·237, 0·613, 0·895
2	0·165, 0·324, 0·375, 0·861
3	0·223, 0·232, 0·322, 0·332
4	0·017, 0·071, 0·171, 0·717
5	0·312, 0·327, 0·371, 0·372

B 6–13 Answers will vary.

C
14	3·5	18	11·7
15	3·7	19	13·5
16	4·8	20	15·6
17	8·1		

D
21	15 m	24	48 m
22	18 m	25	16 m
23	16 m	26	11 m

E
27	0·263	29	0·623
28	0·047	30	0·109

F
31	4·235, 4·352, 4·52, 4·53
32	6·041, 6·141, 6·144, 6·4, 6·41
33	0·69, 0·693, 0·936, 0·963, 1·69
34	10·01, 10·011, 10·111, 11·01, 11·11
35	72·344, 72·4, 72·43, 73, 73·42
36	6·048, 6·448, 6·48, 6·804, 6·884

G
37	8·64, 8·6, 9	41	13·26, 13·3, 13
38	2·46, 2·5, 3	42	18·69, 18·7, 19
39	3·03, 3·0, 3	43	3·56, 3·6, 4
40	16·55, 16·6, 17		

Challenge
Answers will vary. Check children measure correctly.

Page 50

Objectives
- Use known facts and place value to consolidate mental multiplication and division.
- Use the relationship between multiplication and division.
- Develop calculator skills and use a calculator effectively.

Differentiation
- Section A revises work covered previously. Check that this is fully understood before children work on Section B. Discuss strategies for selecting the correct questions to give the answers needed in the *Challenge*.
- Do not use a calculator for the *Challenge*.

Answers

A
1	yellow	7	yellow
2	purple	8	pink
3	blue	9	purple
4	blue	10	pink
5	red	11	grey
6	pink		

B
12	42·3	22	689·2
13	689	23	3726
14	21·25	24	3·8
15	4630	25	45·91
16	4690	26	0·046
17	324	27	0·490
18	185·2	28	0·068
19	34·8	29	2·9
20	1·1	30	12·648
21	33·2	31	0·029

Challenge
Check children play the game correctly.

$62 \div 100 = 0·62$

$12·4 \div 2 = 6·2$

$2·25 \times 8 = 18$

$180 \div 1000 = 0·18$

$1·89 \times 100 = 189$

$19·8 \div 100 = 0·198$

$0·33 \times 6 = 1·98$

$18\,000 \div 10 = 1800$

$44·4 \times 4 = 177·6$

$1·767 \times 1000 = 1767$

$3·26 \times 50 = 163$

$2·3 \times 500 = 1150$

$1·15 \times 100 = 115$

$85 \div 100 = 0·85$

$425 \div 50 = 8·5$

$2·1 \times 9 = 18·9$

Page 51

Objectives
- Use the relationship between multiplication and division.
- Express a quotient as a fraction, or as a decimal rounded to one decimal place.
- Develop calculator skills and use a calculator effectively.

Differentiation
↺ Look back at Section D before starting the *Challenge*.
♠ Write a multiplication that gives the answer: 72·5; 45·3; 84·2; etc. and write three other facts linked to each number statement. In the *Challenge*, if a division leaves no remainder, the player removes one of their counters from one of the boxes.

Answers

A
1. $7 \times 4·4 = 30·8$, $30·8 \div 7 = 4·4$, $30·8 \div 4·4 = 7$
2. $7 \times 6·3 = 44·1$, $44·1 \div 7 = 6·3$, $44·1 \div 6·3 = 7$
3. $4 \times 4·8 = 19·2$, $19·2 \div 4 = 4·8$, $19·2 \div 4·8 = 4$
4. $9·8 \times 7 = 68·6$, $68·6 \div 7 = 9·8$, $68·8 \div 9·8 = 7$
5. $19·3 \times 5 = 96·5$, $96·5 \div 5 = 19·3$, $96·5 \div 19·3 = 5$
6. $27·4 \times 8 = 219·2$, $219·2 \div 8 = 27·4$, $219·2 \div 27·4 = 8$
7. $66·6 \times 9 = 599·4$, $599·4 \div 9 = 66·6$, $599·4 \div 66·6 = 9$

B
8. $9\frac{1}{7}$
9. $5\frac{3}{10}$
10. $8\frac{5}{8}$
11. $9\frac{1}{5}$
12. $8\frac{1}{4}$
13. $35\frac{1}{2}$
14. $11\frac{4}{9}$

C
15. 0·25
16. 0·125
17. 0·375
18. 0·75
19. 0·45
20. 0·625
21. 0·15
22. 0·875
23. 0·22

D
24. 16·25
25. 13·75
26. 9·4
27. 8·6
28. 5·25
29. 12·6
30. 10·375
31. 3·9
32. 5·875
33. 2·6
34. 18·375

E
35. 52·9
36. 40·9
37. 40·8
38. 12·6
39. 80·3
40. 15·2
41. 11·9
42. 2·6
43. 5·2

F
44. correct
45. wrong, $323 \div 8 = 40·375$
46. wrong, $515 \div 4 = 128·75$
47. correct
48. wrong, $211 \div 5 = 42·2$
49. wrong, $379 \div 20 = 18·95$

Challenge
Check children play the game correctly.

Page 52

Objectives
- Develop calculator skills and use a calculator effectively.
- Express a quotient as a fraction, or as a decimal rounded to one decimal place. Divide £ and p by a 2-digit number to give £ and p. Round up or down after division depending on context.
- Use the relationship between multiplication and division.

Differentiation
↺ In section B children should attempt to find the answer to the nearest whole number by using the chunking method. Use a calculator to find the answer to one decimal place. Work in pairs to check the answers and discuss why using the inverse operation does not result in a whole number answer. Work in pairs for Section C.
♠ Attempt questions 16, 17 and 18 without using a calculator. Use a calculator to check the answers.

Answers

A
1. 34, 34·1
2. 154, 153·7
3. 46, 46·3
4. 45, 45·3
5. 14, 14·3
6. 26, 25·7

B

		Estimate	Answer (to nearest whole number)	Answer (to 1 decimal place)
7	$527 \div 18$	25	29	29·3
8	$345 \div 19$	15	18	18·2
9	$543 \div 29$	17	19	18·7
10	$511 \div 13$	50	39	39·3
11	$427 \div 15$	20	28	28·5
12	$573 \div 49$	12	12	11·7

C
13. $7000 \div 1217 = 5·8$, Ann Tartic can buy 5 tickets.
14. $517 \div 65 = 7·95$, 8 photo albums are needed.
15. $£242·25 \div 19 = £12·75$, each ticket costs £12·75.
16. $£6177 \div 29 = £213$, the trip costs £213 for each child.
17. $100 - (17 \times 4) = 32$, $32 \div 8·5 = 3·8$, they can take 3 children.
18. $1\,000\,000 \div 515 = 1941·7$, 1942 performances.

Challenge
Answers will vary.

Page 53

Objectives
- Understand and use the relationship between the four operations, and the principles (not the names) of the arithmetic laws.
- Use brackets.
- Use factors.

Differentiation
- Use a calculator for Section D. Use a calculator for the *Challenge*. Discuss strategies for choosing questions that give the highest scoring answers.
- For the *Challenge* do not use a calculator to answer the questions. Check each answer with a calculator and if the answer is incorrect, no points are scored.

Answers

A
1 *24 x 18 = 6 x 4 x 6 x 3 = 36 x 12 = 432*
2 $16 \times 32 = 4 \times 4 \times 4 \times 8 = 64 \times 8 = 512$
3 $28 \times 18 = 4 \times 7 \times 3 \times 6 = 24 \times 21 = 504$
4 $40 \times 36 = 5 \times 8 \times 6 \times 6 = 30 \times 48 = 1440$
5 $64 \times 24 = 8 \times 8 \times 4 \times 6 = 48 \times 32 = 1536$
6 $12 \times 48 = 3 \times 4 \times 6 \times 8 = 18 \times 32 = 576$
7 $42 \times 14 = 6 \times 7 \times 2 \times 7 = 12 \times 49 = 588$
8 $30 \times 56 = 5 \times 6 \times 7 \times 8 = 35 \times 48 = 1680$
9 $88 \times 8 = 8 \times 11 \times 2 \times 4 = 16 \times 44 = 704$
10 $72 \times 12 = 8 \times 9 \times 3 \times 4 = 24 \times 36 = 864$

B
11 66   15 97
12 47   16 6
13 93   17 99
14 35

C
18–24 Answers will vary.

D
25 40   30 23
26 637   31 2·3
27 45   32 8·7
28 36   33 1·6
29 5·68

Challenge

Check children play the game correctly.

$6 \times (9 + 8) = 102$
$6 \times (9 + 8) = 102$
$250 \div 20 = 12·5$
$783 \div 45 = 17·4$
$36 \times 9 = 324$
$12·8 \times 8·5 = 108·8$
$330 \div 40 = 8·25$

$418·88 \div 52·36 = 8$
$450 \div 40 = 11·25$
$10·85 \times 8 = 86·8$
$(3·3 + 9·5) \times 6 = 76·8$
$490 \div 50 = 9·8$
$17·6 \times 3·7 = 65·12$
$4·37 \times 32 = 139·84$

Page 54

Objective
- Extend written methods to: short division of TU or HTU by U (mixed number answer); short division of numbers involving decimals.

Differentiation
- Work through the first one or two examples before children work on Section B.
- In Section C use a mental method to work out as many answers as possible. Extend the *Challenge* by changing the clues to send the ship to a different port.

Answers

A
1 *49 r 4*   5 123 r 5
2 84 r 2   6 109 r 1
3 86 r 3   7 93 r 2
4 171 r 2

B
8 $73\frac{3}{4}$ 13 $43\frac{5}{6}$
9 $61\frac{1}{3}$ 14 $50\frac{1}{3}$
10 $72\frac{4}{7}$ 15 $120\frac{4}{5}$
11 $79\frac{1}{8}$ 16 $46\frac{3}{8}$
12 $135\frac{1}{4}$ 17 $255\frac{2}{3}$

C
18 Each ticket costs £11·50.
19 Each person pays £310·50.
20 Kai pays £105·25.
21 Each person receives £33·50.
22 You will save £18·75.
23 Each ticket costs £21·52.

Challenge

$284 \div 5 = 56·8$, $65 \div 4 = 16·25$, $514 \div 8 = 64·25$, $492 \div 5 = 98·4$, $103·6 \div 8 = 12·95$, $58·5 \div 9 = 6·5$, $53·45 \div 5 = 10·69$, $365 \div 4 = 91·25$, $63·5 \div 5 = 12·7$

The ship is sailing to Malta.

Page 55

Objective
- Extend written methods to: long multiplication of a 3-digit by a 2-digit integer; division of HTU by TU (long division, whole-number answer).

Differentiation
↻ Work in pairs for the *Challenge*. Keep a running score for the digit total. How many turns are needed to reach a digit total of 100? Can you beat the record?

♠ Estimate the answers in Section E before solving the problems.

Answers

A
1	3432	4	9548
2	4572	5	20 056
3	8184	6	14 357

B
7	$153 \times 22 = 3366$	9	$152 \times 36 = 5472$
8	$222 \times 17 = 3774$	10	$286 \times 34 = 9724$

C
11	$792 \div 24 = 33$	14	$936 \div 36 = 26$
12	$910 \div 26 = 35$	15	$798 \div 21 = 38$
13	$731 \div 43 = 17$	16	$966 \div 23 = 42$

D
17	$952 \div 28 = 34$	19	$756 \div 28 = 27$
18	$702 \div 18 = 39$	20	$928 \div 32 = 29$

E
21	11 730 pins	25	148 hours
22	£12 052	26	26 miles
23	24 596 km	27	584 boxes
24	£27		

Challenge
Check children play the game correctly.

Page 56

Resources
- a calculator
- two sets of 20 counters
- a partner

Objectives
- Develop calculator skills and use a calculator effectively.
- Extend written methods to long multiplication of a 3-digit by a 2-digit integer, division of HTU by TU (long division, whole-number answer), short division of TU or HTU by U (mixed number answer) and short division of numbers involving decimals.
- Use closely related facts.

Differentiation
↻ Check that the children understand the scoring system.

♠ Change some of the questions but still resulting in the same answers.

Answers

1. $4 \cdot 62 \times 100 = 462$
2. $^-11 - 16 = {}^-27$
3. $315 \div 7 = 45$
4. $607 \cdot 2 \div 46 = 13 \cdot 2$
5. $16 \cdot 5 \times 6 = 99$
6. $189 \times 21 = 3969$
7. $(17 + 8) \times 13 = 325$
8. $123 \times 34 = 4182$
9. $64 \div 20 = 3 \cdot 2$
10. $137 \times 23 = 3151$
11. $^-42 + 17 = {}^-25$
12. $6 \cdot 931 \times 100 = 693 \cdot 1$
13. $154 \times 26 = 4004$
14. $78 \div 5 = 15 \cdot 6$
15. $264 \times 18 = 4752$
16. $12 - 40 = {}^-28$
17. $3 \cdot 48 \times 50 = 174$
18. $338 \times 12 = 4056$
19. $6 \cdot 9 \div 100 = 0 \cdot 069$
20. $38 \times 14 = 532$
21. $^-18 - 6 = {}^-24$
22. $43 \div 4 = 10 \cdot 75$
23. $720 \div 45 = 16$
24. $9 \div 1000 = 0 \cdot 009$
25. $(4 \times 8) + 7 = 39$
26. $157 \times 29 = 4553$
27. $101 \div 8 = 12 \cdot 625$

Spring term unit 4 Problem solving

Page 57

Objectives
- Choose and use appropriate number operations to solve problems, and appropriate ways of calculating: mental, mental with jottings, written methods, calculator.
- Explain methods and reasoning.
- Check with an equivalent calculation.
- Develop calculator skills and use a calculator effectively.

Differentiation
 Section A checks that children can use all four operations to solve simple word problems, involving numbers and quantities. Check that children can extract the calculations from the problems. Discuss ways that answers can be checked.

Write an email to a friend to explain how to solve the problems in questions 12 and 13.

Answers

A
1. 4 diaries and 4 biros
2. 22 and 23
3. 3 adults and 3 children
4. 79, 80 and 81
5. 162 programmes
6. £227·90
7. £291·50
8. £394·85

9.

Sweets made	Jars needed
10 000	125
25 000	313
120 000	1500
250 000	3125
1 000 000	12 500

10. 303 bars
11. 20 matchsticks
12. 8250 plots
13. £61 875

Challenge
$12 \times 12 \times 12 = 1728$
$12 \times 43 = 516$
$21 \times 43 = 903$
39% of $78 = 30·42$
$78 \times 45 = 3510$
green = 12
purple = 43
light pink = 21
red = 78

$1176 \div 21 = 56$
$18 \times 18 \times 18 = 5832$
$(18 \times 196) \div 56 = 63$
$78 \times 18 = 1404$
$56 \times 21 = 1176$
grey = 45
orange = 56
yellow = 18
brown = 196

red × yellow = $78 \times 18 = 1404$
orange × light pink = $56 \times 21 = 1176$
$1404 > 1176$ so statement is true.

Page 58

Objectives
- Choose and use appropriate number operations to solve word problems involving measures and money including pounds to foreign currencies and vice versa, and appropriate ways of calculating: mental, mental with jottings, written methods, calculator.
- Develop calculator skills and use a calculator effectively.

Differentiation
 If children are using a calculator, check that they can interpret the display when sums of money are involved.

For the *Challenge* children should include a question involving area and others relating to each of the different currencies referred to in Section A. Work out the cost of laying the path at so much per square metre.

Answers

A

Value in:	£10	£40	£100	£350	£1000
1 US dollars	17·50	70	175	612·5	1750
2 Swiss francs	22	88	220	770	2200
3 South African rand	110	440	1100	3850	11 000
4 Maltese lire	6·1	24·4	61	213·5	610
5 Euros	14·2	56·8	142	497	1420

B

6 American Pie Restaurant
Soup £1·14
Chicken Salad £2·86
Chocolate Pie £1·71
Coffee £0·86

7 Zurich Zone
Prawn Cocktail £4·55
Sausages £6·82
Fruit Salad £3·18
Coffee £1·82

8 The Cape Café
Soup £3·15
Fish Dish £5·86
Dessert £3·60
Coffee £2·25

9 The Med
Salad £3·28
Lasagne £7·38
Trifle £4·10
Lemonade £1·31

10 L'Auberge
Hors d'oeuvre £2·11
Fruits de mer £8·80
Ice-cream £2·82
Coffee £1·76

Challenge
a. 68 m, $1190, £680
b. 54 m, 1170 SF, £531·82
c. 100 m, 610 L, £1000
d. Answers will vary.

Page 59

Objective
- Choose and use appropriate number operations to solve problems, and appropriate ways of calculating: mental, mental with jottings, written methods, calculator.

Differentiation
↻ Check that children can extract the calculations from the problems. Work in pairs or small groups for the *Challenge*.

♁ After completing the *Challenge*, change the values of the letters and provide a new set of clues for a partner. Check each of the clues using the inverse operation.

Answers

A

1	263 people	5	£11·15 left
2	1200 matches	6	147
3	45, 21, 42	7	139 children
4	12·9	8	£2·15

Challenge
a = 8, b = 36, c = 2, e = 5, o = 12, r = 9, s = 16, t = 30, u = 11, y = 3

You are a star!

Page 60

Objectives
- Use a fraction as an 'operator' to find fractions of numbers or quantities.
- Begin to convert fractions to decimals using division.
- Develop calculator skills and use a calculator effectively.

Differentiation
↻ Section A checks that children can relate fractions to division. Section B checks that they can relate fractions to their decimal representations. For section F suggest to children that they record each fraction as a decimal fraction rounded to two places of decimals.

♁ Try to answer the questions in Section F without a calculator. Use strategies such as: comparing fractions to one half; comparing fractions with the same numerator.

Answers

A

1	£3	5	£15
2	£3	6	£83
3	£20	7	£12
4	£8	8	£150

B

9	0·3	13	0·25
10	0·5	14	0·8
11	0·9	15	0·7
12	0·4	16	0·75

C

17	$\frac{3}{5} > \frac{4}{10}$	20	$\frac{1}{2} > \frac{2}{5}$
18	$\frac{7}{10} > \frac{3}{5}$	21	$\frac{1}{2} < \frac{3}{5}$
19	$\frac{9}{10} > \frac{4}{5}$	22	$\frac{3}{10} < \frac{3}{5}$

D

23	0·125	27	0·05
24	0·375	28	0·625
25	0·1875	29	0·55
26	0·45	30	0·8125

E

31	0·14	35	0·86
32	0·29	36	0·67
33	0·83	37	0·08
34	0·09		

F

38	$\frac{1}{5}, \frac{1}{4}, \frac{2}{7}, \frac{2}{5}$	42	$\frac{4}{7}, \frac{2}{3}, \frac{7}{10}, \frac{5}{6}$
39	$\frac{3}{8}, \frac{4}{7}, \frac{3}{4}, \frac{5}{6}$	43	$\frac{3}{11}, \frac{3}{10}, \frac{4}{13}, \frac{5}{9}$
40	$\frac{4}{5}, \frac{6}{7}, \frac{7}{8}, \frac{8}{9}$		
41	$\frac{2}{5}, \frac{3}{7}, \frac{3}{5}, \frac{5}{8}$		

G 44-49 Answers will vary.

Challenge
A FRACTION EARLY IS BETTER THAN A LITTLE LATE.

Objectives
- Order fractions by converting them to fractions with a common denominator and position them on a number line.
- Use a fraction as an 'operator' to find fractions of numbers or quantities.

Differentiation
- Use a calculator to confirm the answers in Section A. In the *Challenge* check answers using a calculator.
- Work on the *Challenge* individually and keep a running total of the amount of money collected. How many turns are needed to collect £100; £1000? Can you beat your record?

Answers

A

1	smaller	3	stays the same
2	larger	4	stays the same

B

	Fractions	New denominator	Equivalent fractions
5	$\frac{1}{2}$ $\frac{1}{3}$	6	$\frac{3}{6}$ $\frac{2}{6}$
6	$\frac{1}{4}$ $\frac{1}{3}$	12	$\frac{3}{12}$ $\frac{4}{12}$
7	$\frac{3}{5}$ $\frac{1}{2}$	10	$\frac{6}{10}$ $\frac{5}{10}$
8	$\frac{4}{5}$ $\frac{1}{3}$	15	$\frac{12}{15}$ $\frac{5}{15}$
9	$\frac{9}{10}$ $\frac{3}{4}$	20	$\frac{18}{20}$ $\frac{15}{20}$
10	$\frac{1}{6}$ $\frac{3}{4}$	12	$\frac{2}{12}$ $\frac{9}{12}$
11	$\frac{5}{6}$ $\frac{2}{9}$	18	$\frac{15}{18}$ $\frac{4}{18}$

C

12	$\frac{3}{6}$, $\frac{4}{6}$	16	$\frac{6}{15}$, $\frac{10}{15}$
13	$\frac{9}{12}$, $\frac{4}{12}$	17	$\frac{4}{24}$, $\frac{9}{24}$
14	$\frac{12}{20}$, $\frac{5}{20}$	18	$\frac{10}{45}$, $\frac{36}{45}$
15	$\frac{2}{12}$, $\frac{9}{12}$		

D 19–27

Challenge
Check children play the game correctly.

Objectives
- Change a fraction to the equivalent mixed number.
- Express simple fractions as percentages.
- Find simple percentages of small whole number quantities.
- Begin to convert fractions to decimals using division.
- Develop calculator skills and use a calculator effectively.

Differentiation
- Work on Section D in pairs.
- For the *Challenge* keep a running total. The first player to 1000 wins. Introduce an extra box for the grid and find percentages of 4-digit multiples of 10.

Answers

A

1	24	4	33
2	50	5	72
3	56	6	96

B

7	$\frac{17}{4}$	11	$\frac{43}{8}$
8	$\frac{26}{5}$	12	$\frac{31}{4}$
9	$\frac{17}{5}$	13	$\frac{29}{10}$
10	$\frac{20}{3}$	14	$\frac{29}{6}$

C

15	$5\frac{1}{3}$	19	$1\frac{8}{9}$
16	$3\frac{3}{4}$	20	$2\frac{1}{2}$
17	$3\frac{4}{5}$	21	$4\frac{2}{7}$
18	$3\frac{1}{2}$	22	$8\frac{1}{5}$

D

	Percentage	Fraction	Decimal Fraction
23	10%	$\frac{1}{10}$	0·1
24	50%	$\frac{1}{2}$	0·5
25	25%	$\frac{1}{4}$	0·25
26	47%	$\frac{47}{100}$	0·47
27	93%	$\frac{93}{100}$	0·93
28	36%	$\frac{36}{100} = \frac{9}{25}$	0·36

E

29	£150 000	33	35 girls
30	£175	34	£525
31	330 apples are not bad	35	£15·50
32	140 km	36	44%

Challenge
Check children play the game correctly.

Page 63

Resources
- 2 sets of number cards 1 to 9
- a calculator

Objectives
- Develop calculator skills and use a calculator effectively.
- Find simple percentages of small whole number quantities.
- Use a fraction as an 'operator' to find fractions of numbers or quantities.

Differentiation
- Explain how to work out the percentage calculation or write a 0 in the second and fifth boxes on the first row and remove the two cards showing the number 9.
- Deal the cards one by one and choose into which empty box each card is placed. Once a card is placed it cannot be moved.

Page 64

Objective
- Recognize where a shape will be after a rotation through 90° or 180° about one of its vertices.

Differentiation
- Section A checks that children recognize where a shape will be after reflection in a mirror line parallel to one side (sides not all parallel or perpendicular to the mirror line). Section B checks that they can complete symmetrical patterns with two lines of symmetry at right angles (using squared paper).

Answers

A 1 2

B 3 4

C 5 6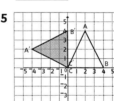

D 7 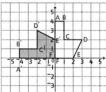 8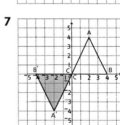

A' = (⁻2,⁻4)   A' = (0,⁻4)   D' = (⁻3,⁻2)
B' = (⁻4,0)   B' = (⁻1,⁻4)   E' = (⁻2,0)
C' = (0,0)   C' = (⁻1,⁻2)   F' = (0,0)

Challenge

a   b   c   d   e

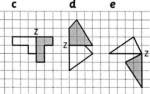

47

Page 65

Objective
- Recognize where a shape will be after reflection: in a mirror line touching the shape at a point (sides of shape not necessarily parallel or perpendicular to the mirror line); in two mirror lines at right angles (sides of shape all parallel or perpendicular to the mirror line).

Differentiation
↺ For questions in Section D, first plot the points and draw the shape on a co-ordinate grid with four quadrants then draw the reflected shapes on the grid. Work in pairs for question 18.

∩ Extend the *Challenge* by drawing a hexagon in the first quadrant of a co-ordinate grid and then reflecting the shape in both the x- and y-axes. Write the co-ordinates of the vertices of all four hexagons.

Answers

A 1 2 3 4

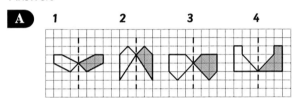

B
5	(4,2)	8	(3,⁻6)
6	(6,3)	9	(1,0)
7	(⁻2,8)	10	(4,⁻7)

C
11	(3,⁻6)	14	(⁻6,⁻2)
12	(2,1)	15	(⁻4,7)
13	(5,7)	16	(0,⁻3)

D
17 2nd quadrant (⁻2,3), (⁻5,3), (⁻2,7)
3rd quadrant (⁻2,⁻3), (⁻5,⁻3), (⁻2,⁻7)
4th quadrant (2,⁻3), (5,⁻3), (2,⁻7)

18 1st quadrant (2,2), (6,2), (5,5), (3,5)
2nd quadrant (⁻2,2), (⁻6,2), (⁻5,5), (⁻3,5)
3rd quadrant (⁻2,⁻2), (⁻6,⁻2), (⁻5,⁻5), (⁻3,⁻5)

Challenge
a Reflecting point (x,y) in x axis gives point (x,⁻y).
Reflecting point (x,y) in y axis gives point (⁻x,y).
Reflecting point (x,y) in x axis and then y axis gives point (⁻x,⁻y).

b Answers will vary.

Page 66

Objective
- Recognize where a shape will be after reflection: in a mirror line (sides of shape not necessarily parallel or perpendicular to the mirror line); in two mirror lines at right angles (sides of shape parallel or perpendicular to the mirror line).

Differentiation
↺ For section A work in pairs. Check reflections using a mirror.

∩ Section C extends the work to recognizing where a shape will be after reflection in two mirror lines at right angles (sides of shape not parallel or perpendicular to the mirror line).

Answers

A 1 2

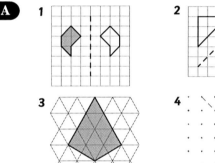

3 4

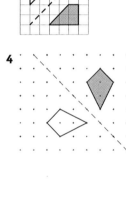

B
5 reflection in x axis
6 rotation 180° centre (0,0)
7 rotation 90° anti-clockwise, centre (0,0)

C 8

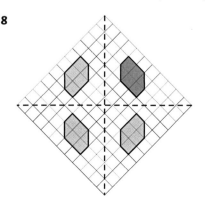

Challenge
Answers will vary.

Page 67

Answers

A
1	7 tenths
2	3 units
3	3 hundredths

4	9 hundredths
5	I hundredth
6	8 tenths

B
7	2·9
8	3·9
9	4·1

10	6·9
11	4·0

C
12	3·28
13	5·97
14	7·05

15	3·83
16	6·83

D
17	$6\frac{4}{7}$
18	$5\frac{9}{10}$
19	$7\frac{3}{5}$
20	$40\frac{1}{2}$

21	$18\frac{1}{4}$
22	$20\frac{1}{5}$
23	$12\frac{1}{8}$

E
24	$78\frac{2}{5}$
25	$68\frac{5}{6}$
26	$24\frac{2}{9}$
27	$89\frac{1}{2}$
28	$55\frac{1}{2}$
29	4662

30	8416
31	9744
32	11 102
33	7056
34	11 886

F
35	90 roses
36	25 and 26
37	800 pins

G
38	0·14
39	0·83
40	0·27

41	0·78
42	0·67
43	0·62

H
44	$4\frac{1}{4}$
45	$1\frac{7}{9}$
46	$4\frac{1}{3}$
47	$3\frac{4}{7}$

48	$4\frac{1}{4}$
49	$7\frac{8}{9}$
50	$8\frac{1}{3}$

I
51	£105
52	£105
53	£504
54	£147

55	£144
56	£841·50
57	£412·50

J

58 59 60

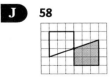
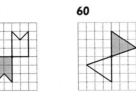

Page 68

Objectives
- Use known number facts and place value to consolidate mental addition/subtraction.
- Extend written methods to column addition and subtraction of numbers involving decimals.
- Explain methods and reasoning.

Differentiation

◐ Section A checks that children can add/subtract two integers less than 10 000. Work through an example before children undertake the *Challenge*.

◑ Work out mentally answers for Section E.

Answers

A
1	3901
2	7442
3	2607
4	1409

5	6830
6	12 294
7	13 583
8	2316

B
9	11·21
10	5·07
11	3·69
12	31·23

13	18·02
14	4·86
15	4·46
16	2·39

C
17–22	Answers will vary.

D
23	*12·52*
24	11·58

25	11·68
26	10·46

E
27	101·4
28	798·6

29	98·26
30	5000

Challenge
Check children play the game correctly.

Page 69

Objectives
- Identify and use appropriate number operations (including combinations of operations) to solve word problems involving numbers and quantities.
- Explain methods and reasoning.
- Estimate by approximating then check result.
- Extend written methods to column addition and subtraction of numbers involving decimals.

Differentiation
 Check that children can extract the calculation from each problem. Work in pairs for the *Challenge*.

 In the *Challenge* use only numbers to two decimal places when children make up their own code.

Answers

A

1	£28·55	5	25·61 kg
2	12·41 m of string	6	8·5
3	£3·81	7	£26·60 left
4	97p	8	£37·28 left

B

	1st number	2nd number	sum	1st number minus 2nd number
9	16	2	18	4
10	19	4	23	15
11	22	8	30	14
12	4·7	18·9	23·6	⁻14·2
13	13·5	6·6	20·1	6·9
14	7	⁻6	1	13
15	3	⁻1	2	4
16	4	⁻3	1	7
17	8·4	⁻1·6	6·8	10

Challenge

19·81 − 6·95 = 12·86 A 　　117·93 − 84·26 = 33·67 R
37·26 − 18·57 = 18·69 B 　　112·81 − 64·9 = 47·91 T
45·76 − 26·8 = 18·96 I 　　123·45 − 54·98 = 68·47 O
39·72 − 19·65 = 20·07 G 　　49·29 + 112·16 = 161·45 I
32·92 − 1·85 = 31·07 T 　　219·87 + 116·38 = 336·25 S
11·64 + 19·83 = 31·47 O 　　423·8 − 62·9 = 360·9 E

In the crate there is: A BIG TORTOISE.

Page 70

Objectives
- Extend written methods to column addition and subtraction of numbers involving decimals.
- Check with the inverse operation when using a calculator.
- Estimate by approximating then check result.

Differentiation
 Use a calculator for work in Sections A and B. Work with the children to agree the rules for the *Challenge*.

After devising the rules for the *Challenge* and playing the game, discuss with a partner how the rules can be improved to make the game more exciting.

Answers

A　1

2·6	1·2	2·2
1·6	2	2·4
1·8	2·8	1·4

2

5·28	0·66	3·96
1·98	3·3	4·62
2·64	5·94	1·32

3

5·28	16·72	17·6	7·92
14·96	10·56	9·68	12·32
11·44	14·08	13·2	8·8
15·84	6·16	7·04	18·48

B

4	10·29	6	25	8	41
5	39·1	7	14·95	9	43·76

C

10	166·06	13	606·5	15	21·93
11	663·95	14	0·884	16	93·7
12	107·4				

Challenge
Check children play the game correctly.

Difference between 2 odd numbers is **even**.
Sum of an odd number of odd numbers is **odd**.
Product of 2 even numbers is **even**.
Sum of 2 or more even numbers is **even**.
Sum of an odd and an even number is **odd**.
Product of 2 odd numbers is **odd**.
Difference between 2 even numbers is **even**.
Difference between an even and an odd number is **odd**.
Sum of an even number of odd numbers is **even**.
Product of an odd and an even number is **even**.
Difference between an odd and an even number is **odd**.
Sum of even and odd numbers is **odd**.

Page 71

Objectives
- Recognize and estimate angles.
- Use a protractor to measure and draw acute and obtuse angles to the nearest degree.
- Check that the sum of the angles in a triangle is 180°.
- Calculate angles in a triangle or around a point.

Differentiation

↻ Section A checks that the children understand area measured in square centimetres. Check that they use the formula 'length times breadth' when finding the area of a rectangle. Use an overhead projector to demonstrate how to measure angles to the nearest degree and how to draw a given angle.

↻ After working on the *Challenge* make a general statement about the sum of the angles in: a triangle; a quadrilateral.

Answers

A 1 60 cm² 3 92 cm²
  2 77 cm² 4 177 cm²

B Estimates will vary. 7 obtuse
  5 acute 8 acute
  6 acute 9 obtuse

10	Angle	A	B	C	D	E
	To nearest 1°	55°	72°	116°	24°	151°

C 11-16 Answers will vary.

D 17 23° 19 36°
  18 146° 20 48°

Challenge
Angles in a quadrilateral add up to 360°.

Page 72

Objectives
- Check that the sum of the angles in a triangle is 180°.
- Calculate angles in a triangle or around a point.
- Describe and visualize properties of solid shapes such as parallel or perpendicular faces or edges.
- Visualize 3D shapes from 2D drawings and identify different nets for a closed cube.

Differentiation

↻ Work in pairs or as a group for Section C.

↻ Extend the *Challenge* by asking children to devise a simple angle code of their own.

Answers

A 1–4 Answers will vary.

B 5 80°
  6 35°
  7 50°
  8 75°
  9 315°
  10 70°
  11 120°

C 12 no
  13 no
  14 yes
  15 no
  16 yes
  17 yes

Challenge
a = 40°, b = 44°, c = 47°, e = 56°, n = 66°, o = 24°, s = 153°, t = 75°, u = 98°, y = 151°
Can a cute baby be obtuse?

Page 73

Objectives
- Describe and visualize properties of solid shapes such as parallel or perpendicular faces or edges.
- Visualize 3D shapes from 2D drawings and identify different nets for a closed cube.
- Calculate the perimeter and area of simple compound shapes that can be split into rectangles.

Differentiation
☻ Work in pairs for the *Challenge*.
♠ Extend the *Challenge* by changing the area of land to 48m^2. Question c then becomes a perimeter of 32 m and question d becomes a perimeter of 44 m.

Answers

A
1   6
2   Answers will vary.

B
3
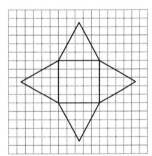

C
4   *perimeter 34 m, area 52 m^2*
5   perimeter 38 m, area 48 m^2
6   perimeter 34 m, area 48 m^2
7   perimeter 38 m, area 56 m^2
8   perimeter 56 m, area 72 m^2
9   perimeter 52 m, area 48 m^2
10   perimeter 34 m, area 40 m^2
11   perimeter 96 m, area 174 m^2

Challenge
a   rectangle 6 m × 6 m, perimeter = 24 m
b   rectangle 36 m × 1 m, perimeter = 74 m
c   rectangle 3 m × 12 m
d   rectangle 2 m × 18 m
e   rectangle 4 m × 9 m

Page 74

Resources
- a protractor
- a calculator
- two sets of 10 counters
- a partner

Objectives
- Estimate by approximating then check result.
- Use known number facts and place value to consolidate mental addition/subtraction.
- Use a protractor to measure and draw acute and obtuse angles to the nearest degree.
- Extend written methods to column addition and subtraction of numbers involving decimals.

Differentiation
☻ Work out strategies to decide which player has the closer estimate.
♠ Extend the *Challenge* by making the winner the first player to place eight counters on the grid. Take turns to roll a dice to determine the move around the track.

Answers

Clockwise from top:

$$125.42 - 39.87 = 85.55$$

$$596.8 + 237.8 = 834.6$$

$$3629.12 - 1148.79 = 2480.33$$

118°

2693 − 867 = 1826
131.26 − 67.85 = 63.41
37°
136°
217°

$$16.42 + 17.98 = 34.4$$

(25.3 − 16.8) × (11.6 − 5.4) = 52.7
3.79 × 7 = 26.53
54°
78°

114.68 − 19.76 = 94.92
15°

Page 75

Objectives
- Use, read and write standard metric units (m, cm, mm, kg, g, l, cl, ml) of length, mass and capacity, including their abbreviations, and relationships between them.
- Convert smaller to larger units (e.g. cm or mm to m, g to kg) and vice versa.
- Know rough equivalents of lb and kg, oz and g, miles and km, litres and pints or gallons.
- Identify and use appropriate number operations (including combinations of operations) to solve word problems involving numbers and quantities based on 'real life', money or measures, using one or more steps.
- Suggest suitable units to estimate or measure length, mass or capacity.

Differentiation
◑ Sections A, B and C check previous work covered on using, reading and writing standard metric units and converting smaller to larger units and vice versa. In Section E check that children can extract the calculation from the problem.

◐ Extend the *Challenge* by keeping a running total in kg. The first player to reach 10 kg is the winner.

Answers

A
1 3·61 m   3 4·09 m
2 4·38 m   4 12·60 m

B
5 500 ml   7 2100 ml
6 750 ml   8 3600 ml

C
9 500 g   10 1200 g   11 3800 g

D
12–21 Answers will vary.

E
22 2405 ml (2·405 l)   25 750 g of potatoes for 84p
23 5·5 cm
24 7·9 kg   26 11p for 50 cm

Challenge
Check children play the game correctly

0·1 kg = 100 g	0·5 kg = 500 g	50 g
250 g	0·2 kg = 200 g	600 g
½ kg = 500 g	1¾ kg = 1750 g	2·25 kg = 2250 g
1200 g	1·2 kg = 1200 g	300 g
1·4 kg = 1400 g	700 g	

Page 76

Objectives
- Record estimates and readings from scales to a suitable degree of accuracy.
- Know rough equivalents of lb and kg, oz and g, litres and pints.

Differentiation
◑ Before answering the questions in Section D check that children can read the scales to a suitable degree of accuracy.

◐ Extend the *Challenge* by rewriting other recipes converting from imperial to metric units or vice versa.

Answers

A
1 340 g   4 230 g
2 400 g   5 450 g
3 60 g   6 570 g

B
7 11 oz   10 18 oz
8 10 oz   11 9 oz
9 2 oz   12 18 oz

C
13 1 kg 350 g   16 4 kg 540 g
14 2 kg 270 g   17 910 g
15 1 kg 590 g   18 45 kg 360 g

D
19 8 lb, green arrow
20 10 l, pink arrow
21 1·5 kg, yellow arrow
22 0·5 l, light blue arrow
23 0·5 lb, red arrow
24 5·5 pints, dark blue arrow

Challenge
Using the approximations 1 oz ≈ 30 g and 1 pint ≈ 570 ml:

Cheese and leek soup
60 g butter
360 g leeks
2 onions
60 g flour
855 ml chicken stock
855 ml milk
240 g cheese
freshly ground pepper
180 g yoghurt

Currant buns
240 g self-raising flour
120 g butter
30 g sugar
142·5 ml milk
150 g currants
60 g brown sugar
30 g mixed peel
45 g glacé cherries

Page 77

Objectives
- Identify and use appropriate number operations (including combinations of operations) to solve word problems involving numbers and quantities based on 'real life', money or measures, using one or more steps and calculating percentages such as V.A.T.
- Record estimates and readings from scales to a suitable degree of accuracy.

Differentiation
- Extend the *Challenge* by asking children to work out the cost of V.A.T. on a range of prices.

Answers

A
1	£2·86	6	45p
2	£2·56	7	£1·60
3	£1·92	8	24p
4	76p	9	£2·08
5	£3·36	10	£34·20

B
- 11 960 g flour, 160 g butter, 800 ml milk, 400 g sugar
- 12 £1·30
- 13 £2·08
- 14 £3·12

C
- 15 130 km
- 16 3 hours
- 17 25 km
- 18 13:30 or 1:30 p.m.
- 19 70 km
- 20 Clive travelled further between 12:00 and 13:00.
- 21 Answers will vary.

Challenge
$17\frac{1}{2}$% £40 = £7
15% of £50 = £7·50
$12\frac{1}{2}$% of £80 = £10
$17\frac{1}{2}$% of £70 = £12·25
25% of £60 = £15
5% of £400 = £20
90% of £30 = £27
40% of £110 = £44

Page 78

Objective
- Solve simple problems involving ratio and proportion.

Differentiation
- Questions 1 to 3 check that children can solve simple problems involving ratio.
- Extend the *Challenge* by drawing on centimetre-squared paper a rectangle with an area of 24 cm^2. Colour the rectangle red and blue so that the ratio of red to blue squares is 5 to 3. Repeat with other rectangles using different ratios.

Answers

A
- 1 72
- 2 6
- 3 5:1

B
- 4 1:3
- 5 1:4
- 6 1:12
- 7 1:3
- 8 4:3
- 9 4:1

C
- 10 60 ml
- 11 350 ml
- 12 150 ml
- 13 350 ml
- 14 orange juice 165 ml lemonade 385 ml
- 15

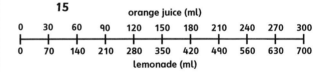

	orange juice (ml)									
0	30	60	90	120	150	180	210	240	270	300
0	70	140	210	280	350	420	490	560	630	700
	lemonade (ml)									

Challenge
- **a** 18 red squares, 6 blue squares
- **b** 6 blue squares, 9 red squares
- **c** 20 red squares, 8 blue squares

Page 79

Objectives
- Solve simple problems involving ratio and proportion.
- Solve a problem by representing, extracting and interpreting data in tables, graphs, charts and diagrams, including those generated by a computer, for example: line graphs; frequency tables.

Differentiation
↻ Check that the children can understand and use the language of proportion and understand the difference between ratio and proportion.

♠ Extend the *Challenge* by drawing conversion graphs for other currencies using current information from newspapers or the internet. For each graph write questions for a partner.

Answers

A
1	$\frac{1}{5}$	3	$\frac{9}{10}$	5	$\frac{1}{4}$
2	$\frac{4}{5}$	4	$\frac{3}{10}$		

B
6	$\frac{4}{5}$	8	$\frac{7}{10}$
7	$\frac{1}{10}$	9	$\frac{3}{4}$

C
10	6 20p coins	13	£31·20
11	30 £1 coins	14	£18·00
12	£1·20	15	20 boys

D   16   Conversion graph (pounds/Australian dollars)

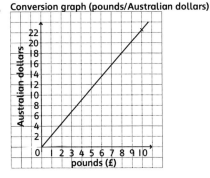

17   Questions will vary.

Challenge
Conversion graph (South African rand/pounds)

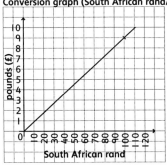

Questions will vary.

Page 80

Objectives
- Solve simple problems involving ratio and proportion.
- Solve a problem by representing, extracting and interpreting data in tables, graphs, charts and diagrams, including those generated by a computer, for example: line graphs; frequency tables and bar charts with grouped discrete data.

Differentiation
↻ Check that the children are able to extract information from the pie charts in Section B and work in pairs or as a group.

♠ Extend the work in Section B by constructing a pie chart to show the favourite colours of 12 children in the class.

Answers

A
1	22 days
2	74 days
3	0 days
4	2 days
5	very hot weather
6	On $\frac{1}{9}$ of the days.

B
7	10 robins
8	3 magpies
9	1 sparrow
10	5 crows
11	Bill (15 chaffinches)
12	Bill (10 greenfinches)
13	8 sparrows
14	$\frac{1}{3}$ of the greenfinches were seen by Ann.

Challenge
Answers will vary.

Page 81

Resources
- a dice
- two sets of 9 counters
- a partner

Objective
- Solve simple problems involving proportion.

Page 82

Objectives
- Know and apply simple tests of divisibility. Find simple common multiples.
- Make general statements about odd or even numbers, including the outcome of products.

Differentiation
◖ Section A checks that the children know all the factors of any number less than 100. Section B checks that they know by heart all multiplication facts to 10 × 10. Before working on Sections C and D, carry out some TU × TU calculations. Use some HTU numbers for the *Challenge*.

◗ Extend the work in Section E by finding the lowest common multiples of larger numbers (e.g. 15 and 20; 16 and 40).

Answers

A
1 *1, 2, 4, 8, 16*
2 *1, 2, 3, 6, 9, 18*
3 *1, 2, 4, 5, 10, 20*
4 *1, 2, 3, 4, 6, 8, 12, 24*
5 *1, 2, 3, 4, 6, 9, 12, 18, 36*
6 *1, 2, 4, 5, 8, 10, 16, 20, 40, 80*

B

7	35	10	48	13	64	16	32
8	72	11	49	14	56	17	81
9	54	12	42	15	36		

C

18	odd	21	even	24	even
19	even	22	odd	25	even
20	odd	23	odd		

D

26	4	28	6	30	0	32	9
27	4	29	2	31	0	33	4

E
34 *lcm = 30*   *60, 90, 120, 150*
35 *lcm = 24*   *48, 72, 96, 120*
36 *lcm = 35*   *70, 105, 140, 175*
37 *lcm = 60*   *120, 180, 240, 300*
38 *lcm = 40*   *80, 120, 160, 200*
39 *lcm = 77*   *154, 231, 308, 385*
40 *lcm = 42*   *84, 126, 168, 210*

Challenge

Number	Exactly divisible by									
	2	3	4	5	6	8	9	10	25	100
6345	✗	✔	✗	✔	✗	✗	✔	✗	✗	✗
1725	✗	✔	✗	✔	✗	✗	✗	✗	✔	✗
1233	✗	✔	✗	✗	✗	✗	✔	✗	✗	✗
4800	✔	✔	✔	✔	✔	✔	✗	✔	✔	✔
3456	✔	✔	✔	✗	✔	✔	✔	✗	✗	✗
2952	✔	✔	✔	✗	✔	✔	✔	✗	✗	✗
3575	✗	✗	✗	✔	✗	✗	✗	✗	✔	✗

Page 83

Objectives
- Recognize prime numbers to at least 20.
- Factorize numbers to 100 into prime factors.

Differentiation
↻ Work in pairs or as a group to find prime numbers greater than 20 in Section B.

↻ Extend the *Challenge* by replacing the dice with a set of cards numbered 1 to 9. Write new tracks using 4-digit numbers.

Answers

A 1–8 Answers will vary.

B 9 2, 3, 5, 7, 11, 13, 17, 19, 23, 29, 31, 37, 41, 43, 47, 53, 59, 61, 67, 71, 73, 79, 81, 89, 97

C
10	2 and 5	14	2, 3 and 5
11	2 and 3	15	5 and 7
12	2	16	2, 3 and 7
13	2 and 3	17	2, 3 and 5

D
18	$2 \times 2 \times 7$	22	$2 \times 5 \times 5$
19	$2 \times 2 \times 3 \times 3$	23	$3 \times 3 \times 7$
20	$2 \times 2 \times 2 \times 2 \times 2$	24	$2 \times 2 \times 2 \times 7$
21	$2 \times 2 \times 5 \times 5$		

E
25	2, 3	28	2, 3
26	2	29	2, 7
27	2	30	2, 5

F
31	7	35	4
32	6	36	8
33	4	37	9
34	6		

G
38	42	41	63
39	120	42	120
40	90		

Challenge
Check children play the game correctly.

Page 84

Objectives
- Solve mathematical problems or puzzles, recognize and explain patterns and relationships, generalize and predict.
- Develop from explaining a generalized relationship in words to expressing it in a formula using letters as symbols (e.g. the cost of n articles at 15p each).

Differentiation
↻ Discuss strategies for Sections A and B. Start with some easier questions (e.g. for Section A find 3 consecutive numbers with a sum of: 18; 33; 45. For Section B find 4 consecutive numbers with a sum of: 18; 38; 58). Discuss Section C with the group.

↻ Extend the *Challenge* by creating some 5-section flags.

Answers

A
1	17, 18, 19	5	80, 81, 82
2	21, 22, 23	6	183, 184, 185
3	51, 52, 53	7	208, 209, 210
4	30, 31, 32		

B
8	22, 23, 24, 25	12	58, 59, 60, 61
9	16, 17, 18, 19	13	85, 86, 87, 88
10	40, 41, 42, 43	14	140, 141, 142, 143
11	36, 37, 38, 39		

C
15 sum = a + b + c (or 3a + 3)
16 sum = a + b + c + d + e (or 5a + 10)

D
17 $240 \div 5 = 48$ or $230 \div 5 = 46$ or $220 \div 5 = 44$ or $210 \div 5 = 42$ or $200 \div 5 = 40$
18 $594 \div 9 = 66$
19 $473 \times 7 = 3311$
20 $216 \times 4 = 864$
21 $256 \times 32 = 8192$
22 $24 \times 63 = 1512$
23 $1238 \times 52 = 64\,376$
24 $470 \times 55 = 25\,850$
25 $4064 \div 8 = 508$ or $4464 \div 8 = 558$
26 $37{\cdot}5 \times 26 = 975$
27 $43{\cdot}56 \div 9 = 4{\cdot}84$

Challenge
a **A** 29 (prime, <40, digit total = 11, odd)
   B 54 (>50, even, multiple of 9, <70)
   C 83 (digit total = 11, odd, >80, prime)
   D 90 (multiple of 9, >80, even, 3 is a factor)
   E 81 (square, 3 is a factor, >50, odd)
   F 2 (prime, <40, <70, even)
   G 64 (square, even, >50, <70)
b Answers will vary.

Spring
term

unit 12

Review 4

Summer
term

unit 1

Decimals, fractions, percentages

Page 85

Answers

A
1 15·79
2 9·87
3 14·59
4 13·63

B
5 12·66
6 27·63
7 50·09

C
8 23°
9 137°
10 105°
11 324°

D
12 perimeter = 52 m, area = 99 m²
13 perimeter = 42 m, area = 74 m²
14 perimeter = 62 m, area = 124 m²

E
15 8 glasses
16 the 2 kg box of mushrooms (312·5p/kg versus 320p/kg)
17 $\frac{2}{7}$ of the mixture is orange juice
18 ratio of water: orange juice is 5:2

F
19 30
20 72
21 44
22 80

G
23 2, 3
24 2, 7
25 2
26 2, 5

H
27 8
28 4
29 7
30 18

Page 86

Objectives
- Multiply and divide decimals mentally by 10 or 100 and integers by 1000, and explain the effect.
- Order a set of mixed numbers with up to three decimal places.
- Round a number with two decimal places to the nearest tenth or whole number.

Differentiation
- Sections A and B check that children can relate fractions to their decimal representations. Section C checks that they can recognize the equivalence between percentages and fractions. Check that children can round an integer to the nearest 10, 100 or 1000.
- Change the clues to lead the shark to a different fish.

Answers

A
1	0.16	3	0.4	5	0.75	7	0.8
2	0.3	4	0.28	6	0.11		

B
8	$\frac{7}{10}$	10	$\frac{3}{10}$	12	$\frac{1}{4}$	14	$\frac{3}{4}$
9	$\frac{6}{10}$	11	$\frac{9}{10}$	13	$\frac{1}{10}$		

C
15	20%	18	60%	21	25%
16	70%	19	50%	22	80%
17	90%	20	12%	23	72%

D
24	$\frac{8}{100}$	26	$\frac{1}{10}$	28	$\frac{2}{1000}$	30	$\frac{3}{100}$
25	$\frac{8}{1000}$	27	$\frac{7}{100}$	29	$\frac{9}{10}$		

E
31	36·4	34	1·479	37	4·763
32	0·425	35	375	38	302·4
33	2620	36	0·291	39	641·7

F
40	46·3 > 4·36	44	71·24 < 72·4
41	4·26 < 42·6	45	16·68 < 16·81
42	24·36 < 24·63	46	437 > 436·89
43	11·89 > 8·99		

G
47 7·36, 7·6, 7·63, 73, 73·6
48 1·849, 8·94, 9·48, 18·49, 18·94
49 2·333, 12·3, 23·32, 112·3, 123·2
50 12·641, 14·261, 14·6, 14·61, 16·42
51 6·905, 6·95, 9·06, 9·56, 9·605

H
52	14·9	54	19·4	56	16·6
53	15·5	55	2·6	57	12·5

Challenge
142 ÷ 10 = 14·2, 23·2 × 100 = 2320, 1·64 ÷ 10 = 0·164,
3·69 × 100 = 369, 3·645 × 10 = 36·45, 2·91 ÷ 10 = 0·291,
83·69 × 10 = 836·9, 4·06 ÷ 10 = 0·046

The salmon is in danger from the shark.

Page 87

Objectives
- Reduce a fraction to its simplest form by cancelling common factors.
- Use a fraction as operator to find fractions of numbers or quantities.

Differentiation

☹ Check that children can recognize when two simple fractions are equivalent. Work through one or two examples before children work on Section C. For the *Challenge* use a set of cards numbered 1 to 6.

☺ Extend the *Challenge* by finding a fraction of a 4-digit or a 5-digit number. Change the rules so that the lower score wins the point.

Answers

A

1 $\frac{2}{5} = \frac{4}{10} = \frac{8}{20} = \frac{10}{25}$ 5 $\frac{4}{9} = \frac{12}{27} = \frac{20}{45} = \frac{32}{72}$

2 $\frac{2}{3} = \frac{4}{6} = \frac{8}{12} = \frac{10}{15}$ 6 $\frac{3}{8} = \frac{12}{32} = \frac{15}{40} = \frac{60}{160}$

3 $\frac{3}{10} = \frac{9}{30} = \frac{12}{40} = \frac{27}{90}$ 7 $\frac{2}{11} = \frac{4}{22} = \frac{16}{88} = \frac{200}{1100}$

4 $\frac{2}{7} = \frac{6}{21} = \frac{12}{42} = \frac{20}{70}$ 8 $\frac{5}{9} = \frac{15}{27} = \frac{25}{45} = \frac{5000}{9000}$

B

9   3   12   8

10   7   13   4

11   9

C

14   $\frac{3}{5}$ 19 $\frac{2}{11}$

15   $\frac{3}{10}$ 20 $\frac{4}{17}$

16   $\frac{4}{7}$ 21 $\frac{4}{9}$

17   $\frac{3}{4}$ 22 $\frac{4}{11}$

18   $\frac{2}{5}$

D

23   Amy has £90 altogether.

24   Andy spent £12.

25   Oscar must travel 790 km further.

26   The farmer has 70 sheep.

Challenge

Check children play the game correctly.

Page 88

Objectives
- Understand percentage as the number of parts in every 100.
- Find simple percentages of small whole number quantities.
- Use a calculator effectively.

Differentiation

☹ Check that children can find percentages using a calculator

☺ Extend the *Challenge* by working out how much V.A.T. has been charged on an item when V.A.T. is already included in the price. (E.g. Price incl. V.A.T. = £32. Price without V.A.T. is: £32 ÷ 117·5 × 17·5 = £4·77 to the nearest penny.)

Answers

A

1   0·24, $\frac{6}{25}$ 7   0·72, $\frac{18}{25}$

2   0·32, $\frac{32}{100}$ 8   0·15, $\frac{3}{25}$

3   0·28, $\frac{28}{100}$ 9   0·05, $\frac{1}{20}$

4   0·16, $\frac{4}{25}$ 10   0·12, $\frac{3}{25}$

5   0·48, $\frac{12}{25}$ 11   0·04, $\frac{1}{25}$

6   0·35, $\frac{7}{20}$

B

12   72 miles   14   486 miles

13   162 miles   15   99 miles

C

16   £264   20   £1470

17   £333   21   £17

18   £693   22   £875

19   £312   23   £9060

D

24   28 fish are not roach or perch.

25   The total cost of the car is £4286·70.

26   79% are fruit cakes.

E

27   65%   31   65%

28   36%   32   96%

29   36%   33   86%

30   11%   34   40%

Challenge

a   £1399·83   e   £19·60

b   £993·13   f   £95·90

c   £135·63   g   £220·50

d   £81·38   h   £15·05

Page 89

Objective
- Extend written methods of column addition and subtraction of numbers involving decimals.

Differentiation
- Sections A and B check that children can use column addition and subtraction for two integers less than 10 000. Section C checks that they know by heart all multiplication facts up to 10 × 10. Before working on Section D discuss how to make a sensible estimate.
- Extend the *Challenge* by creating a spider's web for a partner. Include three 'difficult' questions in the web.

Answers

A
1 5091	4 5958
2 8933	5 1945
3 2190	

B
6 2831	9 5428
7 4527	10 7481
8 796	11 4457

C
12 54	17 45
13 32	18 81
14 42	19 56
15 72	20 49
16 64	

D
21 1167	27 344·71
22 35·12	28 40·25
23 2641	29 340·53
24 431·55	30 7011
25 5835	31 382·73
26 3002	32 570·62

Challenge
The spider will catch:

263·29 + 14·6 + 8·24 = 286·13, Fiz

57·6 − 19·87 = 37·73, Hazz

842·6 − 11·94 = 830·66, Liz

602·4 − 39·68 = 562·72, Jazz

7004 − 991 = 6013, Mizz

4011 + 898 = 4909, Bizzy

645·6 + 18·92 + 1·85 = 666·37, Oz

501·61 − 49·96 = 451·65, Buzz

The spider will not catch Tizz, Bazz, Muz and Arthur.

Page 90

Objectives
- Extend written methods to: short multiplication and division of Th HTU by U; short multiplication of numbers involving decimals; long multiplication of a 3-digit by a 2-digit integer.
- Explain methods and reasoning.
- Check results of calculations.

Differentiation
- Check children have completed Section C satisfactorily and have answered questions in Section D correctly before moving on to Sections E and F.
- Give the quotient as a fraction and as a decimal fraction in Section G. Extend the *Challenge* by placing the four cards on a grid showing tens, units, tenths and hundredths. This time cover the tenths or hundredths number with a counter.

Answers

A
1 25692	4 28992	7 29016
2 24822	5 22212	8 31065
3 7970	6 16212	

B
9 25692 ÷ 4 = 6423	10 22212 ÷ 9 = 2468

C
11	10980 ÷ 5 = 2196
12	1220 × 0·9 = 1098
13	21·96 × 5 = 109·80
14	358·4 × 3 = 1075·2
15	10752 ÷ 7 = 1536
16	15·36 × 7 = 107·52
17	358·4 × 0·3 = 107·52
18	219·6 × 0·5 = 109·8
19	10980 ÷ 1220 = 9

D
20 13390	21 5551	22 19462

E
23 51·5 × 26 = 1339	27 427 × 0·13 = 55·51
24 5·26 × 37 = 194·62	28 52·6 × 3·7 = 194·62
25 42·7 × 1·3 = 55·51	29 515 × 260 = 133900
26 51·5 × 2·6 = 133·9	30 52·6 × 370 = 19462

F
31 168 × 4 = 672	34 68 × 5 = 340
32 6·8 × 4 = 27·2	35 6·8 × 0·4 = 2·72
33 68 × 14 = 952	36 68 × 1·4 = 95·2

G
37 1091	39 92	41 96 r 1
38 1058 r 1	40 203 r 2	42 181

Challenge
Check children play the game correctly.

Page 91

Objectives
- Extend written methods to: short multiplication of numbers involving decimals; short division of numbers involving decimals.
- Extend written methods of column addition and subtraction of numbers involving decimals.
- Use a calculator effectively.
- Explain methods and reasoning.

Differentiation
◔ Check that the children understand how to use the information gained in Section A to answer questions in Section B. Work in pairs for the *Challenge*.

◑ Check answers in Sections D and F by using the inverse operation.

Answers

A

1	18	4	34	7	45
2	27	5	32	8	42
3	23	6	46		

B

9	180	11	2·7	13	450
10	230	12	4·2		

C

14	19·6	17	1420	20	5·3
15	6·8	18	6·1	21	1480
16	540	19	710		

D

22   21·46 ÷ 3·7 = 5·8
23   16·575 ÷ 4·25 = 3·9
24   25·024 ÷ 3·68 = 6·8
25   21·97 ÷ 2·6 = 8·45
26   71·68 ÷ 25·6 = 2·8
27   45·243 ÷ 9·9 = 4·57

E

28–32   Answers will vary.

F

33	39·24	39	10·61
34	29·26	40	14·77
35	23·44	41	3·75
36	18·88	42	6·96
37	122·76	43	6·12
38	130·98		

Challenge

a

2·72	12·24	5·44
9·52	6·8	4·08
8·16	1·36	10·88

b

32·88	38·36	10·96
5·48	27·4	49·32
43·84	16·44	21·92

c

13·14	3·65	2·92	10·95
5·11	8·76	9·49	7·3
8·03	5·84	6·57	10·22
4·38	12·41	11·68	2·19

Page 92

Objectives
- Use a protractor to measure and draw angles to the nearest degree.
- Calculate angles in a triangle or around a point.

Differentiation
◔ Section A checks that children understand area measured in square centimetres and that they can use the formula 'length times breadth' for the area of a rectangle. Section B checks that they can calculate angles in a straight line. Work through a practice example before children work on questions 19 to 21. Work in pairs for the *Challenge*.

◑ If you had not known that the green shapes were isosceles triangles, which angles would you have not been able to calculate?

Answers

A

1   44 cm^2
2   300 cm^2
3   60 cm^2

B

4   28°
5   104°
6   44°
7   141°

C

	Fraction of a complete turn	Amount of turn in degrees
8	$\frac{1}{2}$	180°
9	$\frac{1}{3}$	120°
10	$\frac{1}{4}$	90°
11	$\frac{1}{5}$	72°
12	$\frac{1}{6}$	60°
13	$\frac{1}{10}$	36°
14	$\frac{2}{3}$	240°
15	$\frac{3}{4}$	270°

D

16   53 mm
17   15 mm
18   75°, 82°, 133°, 70°

E   Check pupils' drawings are accurate.

19   7·6 cm, 76°, 49°
20   12·8 cm, 39°, 51°
21   6·8 cm, 41°, 77°

Challenge
a = 26°,   b = 64°,   c = 43°,   d = 47°,   e = 73°,
f = 73°,   g = 60°,   h = 60°,   i = 60°,   j = 30°,
k = 60°,   l = 120°,   m = 30°,   n = 60°,   o = 150°

Page 43

Objectives
- Recognize where a shape will be after reflection.
- Recognize where a shape will be after two translations.
- Read and plot co-ordinates in all four quadrants.

Differentiation
⊍ Reflect some simple shapes with sides parallel or perpendicular to the mirror line before working on Section B.

⊙ Extend the work in section C by reflecting shapes of their own in two mirror lines. On a co-ordinate grid, plot four points in the first quadrant to form a quadrilateral. Reflect the quadrilateral in the x-axis and then the y-axis. Record the co-ordinates of the vertices of the reflected shapes.

Answers

A 1 Shapes a, c, e, f have reflective symmetry.

B 2-3

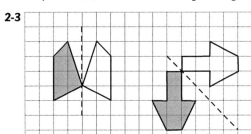

C 4

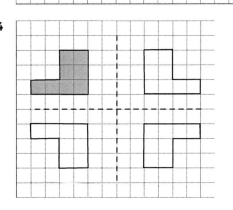

D 5 t, v, z   6 u, w, y

Challenge
a reflect in y-axis

b translate 7 squares right, 1 square down

c translate 4 squares right, 8 squares down

d translate 9 squares right, 8 squares down

e reflect in x-axis

f reflect in x-axis, then in y-axis or reflect in y-axis, then in x-axis

Page 44

Objectives
- Calculate perimeter and area of simple compound shapes that can be split into rectangles.
- Calculate angles in a triangle or around a point.
- Visualize 3D shapes from 2D drawings and identify different nets for a closed cube.

Differentiation
⊙ Extend the work in Section B and D by creating a shape sequence and calculating the perimeter and area of the tenth shape, the thirtieth shape.

Answers

A 1 square, 4 cm × 4 cm

     2-5 Answers will vary.

B 6 *40 cm*   8 80 cm

     7 48 cm   9 800 cm

C 10 area of grass 137 m², perimeter of flower beds 20 m and 24 m

D 11 12 cm²   14 75 cm²   16 1200 cm²

     12 27 cm²   15 300 cm²   17 30 000 cm²

     13 48 cm²

E 18 23°, 157°   20 117°, 63°

     19 136°, 44°   21 66°, 114°

Challenge

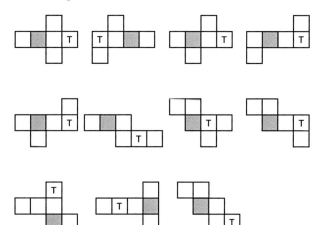

62

Page 95

Resources
- 38 counters

Objectives
- Multiply and divide decimals mentally by 10 or 100.
- Find simple percentages of small whole number quantities.
- Extend written methods of column addition and subtraction of number involving decimals.
- Extend written methods to: short multiplication of numbers involving decimals; short division of numbers involving decimals.

Differentiation
◑ Work in pairs. Check answers with a calculator.

Answers

1	$4.27 \times 10 = 42.7$	**21**	$8307 - 1649 = 6658$
2	$34.3 \times 100 = 3430$	**22**	$2004 - 799 = 1205$
3	$3.45 \times 100 = 345$	**23**	$13.7 + 6.94 + 2.33 = 22.97$
4	$62.36 \times 10 = 623.6$	**24**	$61.73 - 17.87 = 43.86$
5	$4.86 \div 10 = 0.486$	**25**	$49.7 + 18.27 = 67.97$
6	$593.6 \div 100 = 5.936$	**26**	$48.6 - 17.65 = 30.95$
7	$49.31 \div 10 = 4.931$	**27**	$2735 \times 4 = 10\,940$
8	$36.49 \times 100 = 3649$	**28**	$6704 \times 8 = 53\,632$
9	10% of $250 = 25$	**29**	$65.7 \times 5 = 328.5$
10	12% of $200 = 24$	**30**	$42.6 \times 8 = 340.8$
11	15% of $320 = 48$	**31**	$14.7 \times 9 = 132.3$
12	25% of $480 = 120$	**32**	$8305 \div 5 = 1661$
13	$2\frac{1}{2}\%$ of $400 = 10$	**33**	$2367 \div 9 = 263$
14	$12\frac{1}{2}\%$ of $800 = 100$	**34**	$2464 \div 8 = 308$
15	51% of $2000 = 1020$	**35**	$2123 + 63.8 + 19.7 + 6.5 = 2213$
16	35% of $500 = 175$	**36**	$(26.4 + 17.5) \times 11 = 482.9$
17	$4269 + 385 = 4654$	**37**	$3 \times 6.8 = 20.4$
18	$362 + 1457 + 289 = 2108$	**38**	$9 \times 9 \times 10 = 810$
19	$1798 + 497 = 2295$		
20	$2437 - 726 = 1711$		

How long is the red line? 14.3 cm

Page 96

Objective
- Solve a problem by representing, extracting and interpreting data in tables, graphs, charts and diagrams, including those generated by a computer, for example: frequency tables and bar charts with grouped discrete data. Suggest extensions asking, 'What if …?'

Differentiation
◑ Section A revizes previous work on bar charts with grouped discrete data. Help the children to organize their bar charts by discussing the scales needed for each axis paying particular attention to suitable intervals.
◓ Extend the work in Section B by listing the teams in points score order and then finding out if the order would change if 5 points are allocated to children making estimates from: 55 to 65 seconds; 51 to 70 seconds.

Answers

 A

1	How Class 6B estimated the passing of 1 minute
2	28
3	4
4	4
5	$\frac{2}{7}$

B

6	team A scored 9 points
7	team B scored 8 points
8	team C scored 11 points
9	team D scored 10 points
10	team E scored 10 points
11	team F scored 9 points
12	team G scored 9 points

Challenge
Answers will vary.

Page 97

Objective
- Solve a problem by representing, extracting and interpreting data in tables, graphs, charts and diagrams, including those generated by a computer, for example: line graphs; frequency tables.

Differentiation
⊍ Use the line graph to tell the story of Eileen's journey.

⋒ Extend the *Challenge* by predicting how many picture cards and cards that are not picture cards will be in the top 36 cards of a pack. Sketch a pie chart to represent the prediction. Carry out a trial and draw another pie chart to represent the result. Discuss the accuracy of the prediction.

Answers

 A

1	45 miles
2	20 miles
3	25 miles
4	10 miles
5	25 miles
6	40 miles
7	14:00
8	11:45
9	20 miles
10	13:20 and 14:30
11	15:15

 B

12	12
13	6
14	24
15	6

Challenge
Answers will vary.

Page 98

Objectives
- Solve a problem by representing, extracting and interpreting data in tables, graphs, charts and diagrams, including those generated by a computer, for example: line graphs; frequency tables.
- Find the mode and range of a set of data. Begin to find the median and mean of a set of data.
- Identify and use appropriate number operations (including combinations of operations) to solve word problems involving numbers and quantities based on 'real life' or money, using one or more steps, including converting pounds to foreign currency, or vice versa.

Differentiation
⊍ For the *Challenge* help the children to organize their conversion graph by discussing the scales needed for each axis.

⋒ Explain how to check the answers for questions 11 and 12.

Answers

 A

1	HK$15		4	HK$60
2	HK$55		5	HK$100
3	HK$80		6	HK$185

B

7	range = 8, mode = 1 and 4, median = 6, mean = 5
8	range = 6, mode = 7, median = 7, mean = 6
9	range = 8, mode = 2 and 7, median = 7, mean = 5
10	range = 5, mode = 5, median = 6, mean = 6

C

11	John saves £4·06
12	200 coins
13	90p
14	£2·40

Challenge
a   Conversion graph (pounds to baht)

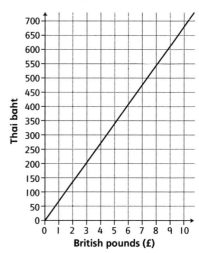

b   Answers will vary.

Page 99

Objectives
- Identify and use appropriate number operations (including combinations of operations) to solve word problems involving numbers and quantities based on 'real life'; money or measures (including time), using one or more steps.
- Convert between imperial and metric units using rough approximations.
- Solve mathematical problems or puzzles, recognize and explain patterns and relationships, generalize and predict. Suggest extensions asking, What if …?'

Differentiation
◑ Section A revizes work previously covered. Work in pairs or as a group for the *Challenge*.
◐ Extend the work in Section B by finding the approximate current temperature in °F, an item in the classroom that is approximately 8 inches long, an object with an approximate mass of 8 oz, etc.

Answers

A
1. 504 phones
2. 2400 boxes

B
3. 18 °F
4. 64 °F
5. 28 °F
6. 46 °F
7. 27 °F
8. 61 °F
9. 12 °C, 47 °F, 1 °C, ⁻3 °C, 22 °F
10. 15 °C, 51 °F, 41 °F, 4 °C, 15 °F

C
11. $3\frac{1}{2}$ inches
12. $4\frac{3}{4}$ inches
13. $1\frac{1}{2}$ inches
14. $4\frac{4}{8}$ inches
15. $2\frac{7}{8}$ inches

D
16. 52p
17. 78p
18. £1·95
19. £2·60
20. £7·80
21. £13
22. £52

Challenge
a. 1·17 m
b. 45 cm
c. 2592 cm² or 0·2592 m²
d. 5457·5 cm² or 0·54575 m²
e. Answers will vary.

Page 100

Objectives
- Identify and use appropriate number operations (including combinations of operations) to solve word problems involving numbers and quantities based on 'real life', money or measures (including time), using one or more steps.
- Solve simple problems involving ratio and proportion.
- Develop from explaining a generalized relationship in words to expressing it in a formula using letters as symbols. E.g. the cost of n articles at 15p.

Differentiation
◑ Before working on Section A work out the quantities required to make: 20 pieces of fudge; 10 pieces of fudge.
◐ Extend the *Challenge* by allowing players to place the counter on a section of their choice and then rolling the dice. The first player with three counters in a row wins. This encourages children to think about the answers they will obtain, e.g. will it be an odd number? Can the answer be less than 5?

Answers

A
1. 420 ml
2. 700 ml
3. 175 ml
4. 1540 ml
5. 20 g
6. 120 g
7. 50 g
8. 5 ml
9. 5 ml
10. 34 minutes
11. Train 2
12. 36 minutes
13. 51 minutes
14. Cranby
15. 59 minutes

Challenge
Check the children play the game correctly.

Page 101

Objectives
- Develop from explaining a generalized relationship in words to expressing it in a formula using letters as symbols. E.g. the cost of n articles at 15p.
- Solve mathematical problems or puzzles, recognize and explain patterns and relationships, generalize and predict.

Differentiation
- Work in pairs for Section C. Use Section D as a group activity.
- Make up some questions like those in Section D for a partner.

Answers

A
1. $2n + 2$
2. $3n + 2$
3. $5n + 2$

B
4. no, the nth term is $3n + 1$, but $99 - 1 = 98$ is not divisible by 3
5. yes, the nth term is $8n$, and 1760 is divisible by 8

C
6-12 red 25, brown 89, yellow 46, orange 20, pink 81, black 3, blue 29

D
13. $m = 9, n = 3$
14. $m = 7, n = 6$
15. $m = 4, n = 8$
16. $m = 4, n = 9$ (or $m = ^-3, n = ^-12$)
17. $m = 4, n = 3$
18. $m = 3, n = 8$ (or $m = ^-\frac{8}{5}, n = ^-15$)
19. $m = 8, n = 9$

Challenge

M = 9	F = 6
R = 7	A = 0
S = 2	H = 8
I = 1	N = 4
T = 5	E = 3

9335 05 583 257309 05 58733 6165334
Meet at the stream at three fifteen.

Page 102

Objectives
- Solve a problem by representing, extracting and interpreting data in tables, graphs, charts and diagrams, including those generated by a computer, for example: line graphs; frequency tables.
- Find the mode and range of a set of data. Begin to find the median and mean of a set of data.
- Identify and use appropriate number operations (including combinations of operations) to solve word problems involving numbers and quantities based on 'real life'; money or measures (including time), using one or more steps.

Differentiation
- Work in pairs.

Answers

1. £9·70
2. £1·70
3. Mr Jolly: range 5, mode 4, median 6, mean 5
Mrs Jolly: range 7, mode 5, median 5, mean 4
Kevin: range 7, mode 3, median 4, mean 5
Ben: range 4, mode 2, median 5, mean 4
Liz: range 7, mode 4, median 4, mean 7
4. Road map £5·16, Ring £33·15, CD £9·54, Football £11·16, Remote control car £17·67
5. Plain flour 175 g, Butter 105 g, Water 7 tablespoons, Jam 14 teaspoons
6. 13 hours 33 minutes
7. 6 hours 42 minutes
8. 311 miles
9. Salcome
10. Stanton
11. Graph B. The distance travelled while stopped is zero so the line on the graph should be horizontal between the times stopped.

Summer term

unit 6

Division, decimals and problem solving

Page 103

Objective
- Solve a problem by extracting and interpreting information presented in tables, graphs and charts.

Differentiation

↻ Section A checks that children can order a set of numbers with the same number of decimal places. Section B checks that they know by heart all multiplication facts up to 10 × 10.

♪ Extend work in Section C by producing an input/output table so that a partner can work out the operation carried out by the machine. The table should include at least two negative numbers.

Answers

A
1 2·46, 2·64, 4·26, 4·62, 6·24
2 1·37, 3·07, 3·17, 3·71, 3·77
3 11·55, 11·59, 11·95, 15·91, 19·15
4 23·24, 23·32, 23·42, 24·23, 24·32
5 19·19, 19·91, 19·99, 20·19, 20·91
6 13·84, 18·33, 18·34, 18·43, 18·44

B
7 63
8 42
9 72
10 49
11 48
12 36
13 56
14 81
15 32

C
16 yellow number + (3 × blue number) = output number
17 (3 × orange number) − (2 × blue number) = output number
18 (3 × pink number) + (2 × blue number) + orange number = output number

Challenge
Check children play the game correctly.

Page 104

Objectives
- Derive quickly division facts corresponding to multiplication tables up to 10 × 10.
- Order a mixed set of numbers with up to three decimal places.
- Solve a problem by extracting and interpreting information presented in tables, graphs and charts.

Differentiation

↻ For Section C discuss how the information should be recorded before undertaking questions 18, 19 and 20.

♪ Extend the work in Section C by devising a points scoring system that would have enabled Kings to win the league in 2004. Extend the *Challenge* by predicting which diagonal will have the higher total and then checking the prediction.

Answers

A
1 45 ÷ 9 = 5, 45 ÷ 5 = 9, 4·5 ÷ 9 = 0·5, 45 ÷ 0·5 = 90, 45 ÷ 0·9 = 50, 4·5 ÷ 5 = 0·9
2 42 ÷ 7 = 6, 42 ÷ 6 = 7, 4·2 ÷ 7 = 0·6, 42 ÷ 0·6 = 70, 42 ÷ 0·7 = 60, 4·2 ÷ 6 = 0·7
3 35 ÷ 7 = 5, 35 ÷ 5 = 7, 3·5 ÷ 7 = 0·5, 35 ÷ 0·5 = 70, 35 ÷ 0·7 = 50, 3·5 ÷ 5 = 0·7
4 32 ÷ 8 = 4, 32 ÷ 4 = 8, 3·2 ÷ 8 = 0·4, 32 ÷ 0·4 = 80, 32 ÷ 0·8 = 40, 3·2 ÷ 4 = 0·8
5 54 ÷ 9 = 6, 54 ÷ 6 = 9, 5·4 ÷ 9 = 0·6, 54 ÷ 0·6 = 90, 54 ÷ 0·9 = 60, 5·4 ÷ 6 = 0·9
6 30 ÷ 6 = 5, 30 ÷ 5 = 6, 3·0 ÷ 6 = 0·5, 30 ÷ 0·5 = 60, 30 ÷ 0·6 = 50, 3·0 ÷ 5 = 0·6
7 27 ÷ 9 = 3, 27 ÷ 3 = 9, 2·7 ÷ 9 = 0·3, 27 ÷ 0·3 = 90, 27 ÷ 0·9 = 30, 2·7 ÷ 3 = 0·9
8 24 ÷ 6 = 4, 24 ÷ 4 = 6, 2·4 ÷ 6 = 0·4, 24 ÷ 0·4 = 60, 24 ÷ 0·6 = 40, 2·4 ÷ 4 = 0·6
9 8 ÷ 1 = 8, 8 ÷ 8 = 1, 0·8 ÷ 1 = 0·8, 8 ÷ 0·8 = 10, 8 ÷ 0·1 = 80, 0·8 ÷ 8 = 0·1
10 60 ÷ 10 = 6, 60 ÷ 6 = 10, 6·0 ÷ 10 = 0·6, 60 ÷ 0·6 = 100, 60 ÷ 1·0 = 60, 6·0 ÷ 6 = 1·0

B
11 3·125, 3·25, 3·52, 3·521, 3·6
12 4·26, 4·263, 4·362, 4·6, 4·65
13 8·2, 8·91, 9·028, 9·182, 9·28
14 11·272, 11·607, 11·651, 11·7, 11·72
15 8·061, 8·16, 8·601, 8·61, 8·66

C
16 win = 3 points, draw = 1 point, loss = 0 points
17 win = 2 points, draw = 1 point, loss = 0 points goal = 1 point
18 Rangers (52), Rovers (40), United (35), Diamonds (27), Valley (12), Kings (9)
19 Rangers (46 points)
20 Valley (20 points)

Challenge
a 1·07
b 1·07
c 2·95
d 1·07
e 9·65
f 8·75
g 6·24
h 9·82
i column 3 (36·67)
j row 1 (22·84)
k Answers will vary.

Page 105

Objectives
- Derive quickly division facts corresponding to multiplication tables up to 10 × 10.
- Solve a problem by extracting and interpreting information presented in tables, graphs and charts.
- Identify and use appropriate number operations (including combinations of operations) to solve word problems involving numbers and quantities based on 'real life', money or measures (including time), using one or more steps, including calculating percentages such as V.A.T.

Differentiation
🔱 Make up some questions for a partner like those in Section A.
🜛 Using the two grids in the *Challenge* make up a new set of rules for a different game.

Answers

 A

1 Banga
2 Goa, Banga
3 £8004
4 Macro
5 Goa
6 Laser £29 610, Macro £11 103·75, Goa £15 792, Dart £17 202, Banga £8223·83
7 Laser £21 420, Macro £8032·5, Goa £11 424, Dart £12 444, Banga £5949·15

Challenge

Check the children play the game correctly.

45 ÷ 0·5 = 90	100 ÷ 25 = 4	6·4 ÷ 8 = 0·8	3·6 ÷ 3·6 = 1	2·8 ÷ 7 = 0·4
36 ÷ 0·9 = 40	5·6 ÷ 8 = 0·7	40 ÷ 8 = 5	1·8 ÷ 9 = 0·2	36 ÷ 6 = 6
81 ÷ 9 = 9	49 ÷ 0·7 = 70	300 ÷ 100 = 3	6·3 ÷ 7 = 0·9	25 ÷ 0·5 = 50
72 ÷ 0·9 = 80	56 ÷ 7 = 8	3·5 ÷ 7 = 0·5	80 ÷ 40 = 2	2·7 ÷ 9 = 0·3
42 ÷ 6 = 7	24 ÷ 1·2 = 20	24 ÷ 0·8 = 30	30 ÷ 0·5 = 60	4·2 ÷ 7 = 0·6

Page 106

Objectives
- Carry out column addition and subtraction of numbers involving decimals.
- Check results of calculations.

Differentiation
🔱 Section A checks that children can use column addition and subtraction for two integers less than 10 000. Work in pairs for the *Challenge* and use a calculator to check line totals.
🜛 Extend the *Challenge* by finding if the square is still magic after adding 1·075 to each number in the first magic square or subtracting 4·86 from every number in the third magic square. Explain the reason.

Answers

A

1	4743	7	11 767	13	3824
2	3907	8	16 665	14	3450
3	9200	9	3076	15	5065
4	8523	10	1859	16	5645
5	6359	11	1216		
6	12 760	12	1109		

B

17	9·131	20	22·351	23	139·404
18	20·137	21	31·223	24	25·948
19	84·63	22	56·907		

C

25	9·282	28	12·752	31	11·855
26	15·089	29	4·706	32	198·249
27	5·217	30	7·726		

D

33 20·137 − 11·63 = 8·507
34 31·223 − 7·02 = 24·203
35 25·948 − 7·3 = 18·648
36 15·089 + 2·861 = 17·95
37 7·594 + 4·706 = 12·3
38 198·249 + 17·951 = 216·3

E

39	14·7 + 6·543	43	6·521 + 7·75
40	13·43 + 7·75	44	13·43 + 8·2
41	6·324 + 6·52	45	6·543 + 6·52
42	15·79 + 14·25		

Challenge

a

13·35	15·575	4·45
2·225	11·125	20·025
17·8	6·675	8·9

b

26·568	3·321	19·926
9·963	16·605	23·247
13·284	29·886	6·642

c

13·35	42·275	44·5	20·025
37·825	26·7	24·475	31·15
28·925	35·6	33·375	22·25
40·05	15·575	17·8	46·725

Page 107

Objective
- Calculate the perimeter and area of simple compound shapes that can be split into rectangles.

Differentiation
- Use an 'L' shaped garden for the *Challenge*.
- Extend the *Challenge* by working out the cost of seeding the lawn if half the garden is lawn and the cost of grass seed is 42p per square metre.

Answers

A
1. $216 \, m^2$
2. $280 \, m^2$
3. $75 \, m^2$
4. £117·60
5. 140 paving slabs
6. $72 \, m$
7. £249·20
8. £268·80
9. Answers will vary.

Challenge
Answers will vary.

Page 108

Objective
- Identify and use appropriate number operations (including combinations of operations) to solve word problems involving numbers and quantities and explain methods and reasoning.

Differentiation
- Discuss the findings from question 8 and consider other nets. For the *Challenge* check children's designs before they make the boxes.
- Extend the *Challenge* by drawing the net of an open box that would hold: 80 Multilink cubes; 108 Multilink cubes.

Answers

A
1. $8 \, cm \times 5 \, cm$, $8 \, cm \times 3 \, cm$, $64 \, cm^2$
2. $4 \, cm \times 4 \, cm$, $4 \, cm \times 2 \, cm$, $2 \, cm \times 6 \, cm$, $36 \, cm^2$
3. $3 \, cm \times 6 \, cm$, $7 \, cm \times 4 \, cm$, $3 \, cm \times 4 \, cm$, $7 \, cm \times 6 \, cm$, $100 \, cm^2$
4. $10 \, m \times 3 \, m$, $2 \, m \times 9 \, m$, $2 \, m \times 3 \, m$, $10 \, m \times 9 \, m$, $144 \, m^2$

B
5. Check boxes have been made correctly.
6. 12 $(3 \times 2 \times 2)$
7. 24 $(6 \times 2 \times 2)$
8. 24 $(3 \times 3 \times 2)$

C
9. $148 \, cm^2$
10. $442 \, cm^2$
11. $340 \, cm^2$
12. $228 \, cm^2$

Challenge
a box could be $1 \times 1 \times 30$, $1 \times 2 \times 15$, $1 \times 3 \times 10$, $1 \times 5 \times 6$, $2 \times 3 \times 5$ (all dimensions in cm)
b box could be $1 \times 1 \times 36$, $1 \times 2 \times 18$, $1 \times 3 \times 12$, $1 \times 4 \times 9$, $1 \times 6 \times 6$, $2 \times 2 \times 9$, $2 \times 3 \times 6$, $3 \times 3 \times 4$ (all dimensions in cm)

Page 109

Objectives
- Understand percentage as the number of parts in every 100 and find simple percentages of whole-number quantities.
- Multiply and divide decimals mentally by 10 or 100 and integers by 1000, and explain the effect.

Differentiation
- Section A checks that children can multiply and divide any positive integer up to 10 000 by 10 or 100 and understand the effect. Section B checks that they can find simple percentages of small whole number quantities. Check that children can find percentages using a calculator before working on Sections G and H. For Section I round prices to the nearest pound. Discuss sensible strategies to tackle the *Challenge*.
- Extend the *Challenge* by working out how many 1s you would write if you wrote every integer from 1 to 1111.

Answers

A
1 420	**4** 1500	**7** 630
2 5600	**5** 64	**8** 80
3 4230	**6** 52	**9** 432

B
10 £3·60	**12** £12	**14** £30	**16** £360
11 £6	**13** £45	**15** £18	**17** £24

C
18 100 times larger	**20** 10 times larger
19 1000 times larger	**21** 100 times larger

D
22 12 notes	**26** 2400 coins
23 24 notes	**27** 12 000 coins
24 120 notes	**28** 120 000 coins
25 240 notes	

E
29 6	**31** 1000	**33** 10
30 0·6	**32** 1000	

F
34 $\frac{2}{5}$	**36** $\frac{3}{20}$	**38** $\frac{17}{50}$
35 $\frac{3}{4}$	**37** $\frac{7}{20}$	**39** $\frac{12}{25}$

G
40 49 g	**42** £30·50	**44** 1100 km
41 13·2 l	**43** 241 miles	**45** 605 ml

H
46 56 km	**48** 2375 cl	**50** 4030 g
47 £1029	**49** £1404	**51** £626

I
52 £5·58	**55** £8999·10	**58** £36·98
53 £98·94	**56** £26·33	**59** £1137·60
54 £270·75	**57** £26·12	

Challenge
1300 (1000 as thousands digits, 100 as hundreds digits, 10 × 10 = 100 as tens digits, 10 × 10 = 100 as units digits)

Page 110

Objective
- Understand percentage as the number of parts in every 100 and find simple percentages of whole-number quantities.

Differentiation
- For Section A use a calculator. Check that children understand how to find the percentages using a calculator. Round prices in Section B to the nearest pound. Work in pairs for questions 10 to 17. Questions 18 to 23 may need to be tackled in a teacher led group. For the *Challenge* children should work in pairs or as a group.
- Extend the *Challenge* by working out what percentage Sam should reduce the price on each item if he only adds 25% to the catalogue prices.

Answers

A
1 £7·99	**4** £63·76
2 £5·36	**5** £136·83
3 £26·61	

B
6 £700	**8** £171·50
7 £405	**9** £120·50

C
10 £23·76	**17** £13·32
11 £308·07	**18** 19p
12 £166·59	**19** £1·56
13 £450·36	**20** £4·17
14 £265·14	**21** £2·85
15 £36·18	**22** £29·45
16 £33·48	**23** 22p

Challenge
All selling prices should be reduced by 25% (26% would result in a loss).

a selling price = £210 + 35% = £283·50
reduce price by 25% = £212·63
profit = £212·63 − £210 = £2·63

b selling price = £155 + 35% = £209·25
reduce price by 25% = £156·94
profit = £156·94 − £155 = £1·94

c selling price = £85·80 + 35% = £115·83
reduce price by 25% = £86·87
profit = £86·87 − £85·80 = £1·07

d selling price = £164 + 35% = £221·40
reduce price by 25% = £166·05
profit = £166·05 − £164 = £2·04

Page 111

Objectives
- Multiply and divide decimals mentally by 10 or 100 and integers by 1000, and explain the effect.
- Solve simple problems involving ratio and proportion.

Differentiation
↻ For Section B draw the enlarged shapes on centimetre squared paper. Work in pairs for Section C.

∩ Extend the *Challenge* by presenting compound shapes that can be split into rectangles but not drawn on squared paper. Give the dimensions of the shapes. Find the perimeter and area of the shapes when the sides are increased in the ratio of 1 to 3, 1 to 5, 1 to 20, etc.

Answers

A
1	£8	7	212 kg
2	£160	8	424 kg
3	80 p	9	40 000 km
4	£800	10	144 000 km
5	4·24 kg	11	97 600 km
6	424 g	12	160 000 km

B
- 13 perimeter 20 cm, area 24 cm^2
- 14 perimeter 30 cm, area 54 cm^2
- 15 perimeter 50 cm, area 150 cm^2

C
16	16 cm^2	20	400 cm^2
17	64 cm^2	21	1600 cm^2
18	100 cm^2	22	40 000 cm^2
19	256 cm^2		

D
- 23 81 cm^2
- 24 72 cm^2

E
25	78 cm	27	260 cm
26	208 cm		

Challenge
a perimeter 88 cm, area 176 cm^2

b

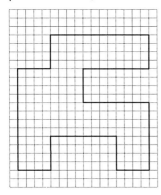

Page 112

Resources
- two sets of 30 counters
- two copies of the game card showing 12 empty sections
- a partner

Objectives
- Carry out column addition and subtraction of numbers involving decimals.
- Derive quickly division facts corresponding to multiplication tables up to 10 × 10.
- Multiply and divide decimals mentally by 10 or 100 and integers by 1000, and explain the effect.
- Understand percentage as the number of parts in every 100 and find simple percentages of whole-number quantities.

Differentiation
↻ Play the game individually. How many questions do you need to answer before you can cover any four answers on your card?

∩ Play the game individually. How many questions do you have to answer to form a straight line of three counters on your card?

Answers

7·274 + 8·39 = 15·664	35 ÷ 0·5 = 70	15% of 380 = 57	14·9 − 6·32 = 8·58	20% of 940 = 188	7·2 ÷ 8 = 0·9
$17\frac{1}{2}$% of 280 = 49	42·61 − 27·94 = 14·67	45 ÷ 0·9 = 50	28·64 + 2·497 = 31·137	110% of 150 = 165	4·5 ÷ 9 = 0·5
26 ÷ 0·5 = 52	40·11 − 9·876 = 30·234	2·1 ÷ 7 = 0·3	60% of 340 = 204	5·6 ÷ 7 = 0·8	35% of 480 = 168
$33\frac{1}{3}$% of 414 = 138	40 ÷ 0·4 = 100	5·4 ÷ 6 = 0·9	4·62 − 1·9 = 2·72	32 ÷ 0·8 = 40	25% of 628 = 157

Page 113

Objectives
- Choose and use appropriate number operations to solve problems, and appropriate ways of calculating: mental, mental with jottings, written methods, calculator.

Differentiation
↻ Sections A, B and C check that children can use a written method for: short multiplication of HTU or U.t by U; long multiplication of TU by TU; short division of HTU by U (with integer remainder). Work through one or two examples before children start work on Section D.

↑ Extend the *Challenge* by using the spider, the kangaroo and the starfish. Find out how they can show numbers, starting at 101, with all three of them contributing to each number (e.g. $101 = (8 \times 8) + (8 \times 5) - 3$).

Answers

A
1	1638
2	2975
3	4120
4	1977
5	5808
6	23·5
7	49·2
8	27·3
9	77·4

B
10 805 12 1664
11 1440 13 1247

C
14 $72\frac{3}{5}$ 16 $69\frac{7}{9}$
15 $235\frac{3}{4}$ 17 $51\frac{5}{7}$

D
18 $5 + 5 - 8$
19 $8 - 5$
20 $8 + 8 + 8 - 5 - 5 - 5 - 5$
21 5
22 $8 + 8 - 5 - 5$
23 8
24 $5 + 5$
25 $5 + 5 + 5$
26 $5 + 5 + 5 + 5$
27 $(5 + 5) \times (5 + 5)$
28 7
29 39
30 54
31 28
32 41
33 22

Challenge
Answers will vary, e.g.

$8 + 8 - 3 - 3 - 3 - 3 - 3 = 1$

$8 - 3 - 3 = 2$

$8 + 8 + 8 - 3 - 3 - 3 - 3 - 3 - 3 - 3 = 3$

$8 + 8 - 3 - 3 - 3 - 3 = 4$

Page 114

Objectives
- Carry out long multiplication of a 3-digit by a 2-digit integer.
- Carry out short multiplication and division of numbers involving decimals
- Factorize numbers into prime factors.
- Develop calculator skills and use a calculator effectively.

Differentiation
↻ Check answers to Sections A and B with the inverse operation using a calculator.

↑ Consider the tables produced after the *Challenge* and discuss what happens as the table goes on and on and whether it will ever end.

Answers

A
1 16 668 3 13 468 5 21 710
2 13 965 4 11 872

B
6 50·88 8 46·30 10 24·56
7 52·15 9 29·58 11 57·95

C
12 22·8 14 7·9 16 8·7
13 5·9 15 5·9 17 7·3

D
18 4 22 25 26 32
19 9 23 36 27 216
20 8 24 125 28 81
21 27 25 256 29 1000

E
30 $2 \times 3 \times 3 \times 3 = 2 \times 3^3$ 36 $2 \times 3 \times 7$
31 $2^2 \times 3 \times 5$ 37 3×5^2
32 $2^3 \times 3$ 38 $2^3 \times 3^2$
33 2^4 39 $2^2 \times 5^2$
34 $2^2 \times 3^2$ 40 $2^3 \times 3 \times 5$
35 $2^3 \times 5$ 41 $2^3 \times 3 \times 5^2$

Challenge
Check children follow the instructions in a–g correctly.

b $64 \, \text{cm}^2$

g

Division	Fraction of whole square to colour	Total area of whole square coloured
1	$\frac{1}{2}$	$32 \, \text{cm}^2$
2	$\frac{1}{4}$	$48 \, \text{cm}^2$
3	$\frac{1}{8}$	$56 \, \text{cm}^2$
4	$\frac{1}{16}$	$60 \, \text{cm}^2$
5	$\frac{1}{32}$	$62 \, \text{cm}^2$
6	$\frac{1}{64}$	$63 \, \text{cm}^2$
7	$\frac{1}{128}$	$63·5 \, \text{cm}^2$

Page 115

Objectives
- Carry out long multiplication of a 3-digit by a 2-digit integer.
- Identify and use appropriate number operations (including combinations of operations) to solve word problems involving numbers and quantities and explain methods and reasoning.
- Choose and use appropriate number operations to solve problems, and appropriate ways of calculating: mental, mental with jottings, written methods, calculator.
- Develop calculator skills and use a calculator effectively.

Differentiation
◑ Check that the children can extract the calculations from the problems. Work in pairs.
◓ Extend the *Challenge* by finding out how many blocks of flats could be built in a year if all the men were working.

Answers

A
1. 4560
2. 27 360
3. 91 200
4. 456 000
5. 1 368 000
6. 1 504 800

B
7. 14 080 fridges
8. 4760 fridges
9. 830 fridges
10. 52 360 fridges

Challenge
a. 80 days
b. 60 days
c. 26 days (25·3)

Page 116

Objectives
- Use a fraction as an 'operator' to find fractions of numbers or quantities, e.g. $\frac{5}{8}$ of 32, $\frac{7}{10}$ of 40, $\frac{9}{100}$ of 400 centimetres.
- Develop calculator skills and use a calculator effectively.

Differentiation
◑ Section A checks that children can relate fractions to division and use division to find simple fractions of numbers and quantities. Discuss the strategies children will use to make the estimations for Section B.
◓ Extend the *Challenge* by devising a similar code for a partner.

Answers

A
1	£4	4	£14	6	£9
2	£30	5	£21	7	£11
3	£11				

B
8. Ivy (£567)
9. Ollie (£483)

C
| 10 | £520 | 12 | £567 | 14 | £492 |
| 11 | £545 | 13 | £492 | 15 | £513 |

Challenge
G = 492
B = 468
Y = 437
O = 385
P = 342
U = 338
F = 306
T = 255
R = 228
V = 209
J = 171
D = 156
L = 99
M = 42
Z = 39

GBY OPUFT RVJDLMZ
FAX NOTES QUICKLY

Page 117

Objectives
- Reduce a fraction to its simplest form by cancelling common factors.
- Develop calculator skills and use a calculator effectively.

Differentiation
U Work in pairs for Section C. If necessary allow a calculator. For the *Challenge* keep a note of fractions chosen from the yellow box so that they are not repeated.

O Extend the *Challenge* by finding in the yellow box: the largest fraction; the smallest fraction. Also list any sets of equivalent fractions.

Answers

A

1	$\frac{5}{6}$	6	$\frac{7}{16}$
2	$\frac{8}{9}$	7	$\frac{5}{9}$
3	$\frac{7}{9}$	8	$\frac{5}{9}$
4	$\frac{4}{5}$	9	$\frac{4}{15}$
5	$\frac{3}{20}$	10	$\frac{5}{8}$

11	$\frac{7}{11}$
12	$\frac{3}{8}$
13	$\frac{3}{16}$
14	$\frac{9}{25}$

B

15	$\frac{1}{3}$	17	$\frac{1}{3}$	19	$\frac{13}{20}$
16	$\frac{3}{4}$	18	$\frac{1}{4}$	20	$\frac{2}{5}$

C

21	$\frac{1}{8}$	23	$\frac{5}{11}$
22	$\frac{7}{8}$	24	$\frac{1}{4}$

D

25	4	27	20
26	8	28	44

E

29	45	31	100
30	60	32	200

Challenge
Check children play the game correctly.

$\frac{162}{216} = \frac{3}{4}$ $\frac{189}{252} = \frac{3}{4}$ $\frac{128}{192} = \frac{2}{3}$ $\frac{192}{480} = \frac{2}{5}$ $\frac{216}{252} = \frac{6}{7}$ $\frac{96}{240} = \frac{2}{5}$ $\frac{256}{320} = \frac{4}{5}$

$\frac{72}{180} = \frac{2}{5}$ $\frac{125}{200} = \frac{5}{8}$ $\frac{175}{250} = \frac{7}{10}$ $\frac{160}{256} = \frac{5}{8}$ $\frac{288}{336} = \frac{6}{7}$ $\frac{99}{363} = \frac{3}{11}$ $\frac{150}{180} = \frac{5}{6}$

$\frac{75}{90} = \frac{5}{6}$ $\frac{275}{330} = \frac{5}{6}$ $\frac{144}{168} = \frac{6}{7}$ $\frac{72}{96} = \frac{3}{4}$ $\frac{140}{252} = \frac{5}{9}$ $\frac{240}{360} = \frac{2}{3}$ $\frac{108}{126} = \frac{6}{7}$

$\frac{80}{144} = \frac{5}{9}$ $\frac{288}{432} = \frac{2}{3}$ $\frac{196}{280} = \frac{7}{10}$ $\frac{175}{210} = \frac{5}{6}$ $\frac{180}{288} = \frac{5}{8}$ $\frac{54}{198} = \frac{3}{11}$ $\frac{56}{80} = \frac{7}{10}$

Page 118

Objective
- Solve simple problems involving ratio and proportion.

Differentiation
U Check that the children understand the difference between ratio and proportion. Work in pairs for the *Challenge*.

O Explain the strategies used to solve some of the problems.

Answers

A 1-7 Answers will vary.

B
- 8 54 apples
- 9 72 kg
- 10 5:8
- 11 group 1 = 6 children, group 2 = 9 children, group 3 = 10 children, group 4 = 5 children
- 12 17 kg (16 from 71 kg and 1 from 34 kg) There will be 55 kg of flour in the orange container and 33 kg of flour in the blue container, a ratio of 55:33 = 5:3.

Challenge
Answers will vary.

Page 119

Resources
- a dice
- two sets of 6 counters
- two score sheets
- a partner

Objectives
- Carry out short multiplication and division of numbers involving decimals.
- Choose and use appropriate number operations to solve problems, and appropriate ways of calculating: mental, mental with jottings, written methods, calculator.
- Use a fraction as an 'operator' to find fractions of numbers or quantities.

Differentiation
◔ Discuss how to record information on the score sheets. Work in teams of two. One child works out the answer to each question and the second child keeps a running total of the money available and uses a calculator to check each answer.

Answers

$\frac{1}{9}$ of £423 = £47, $\frac{3}{8}$ of £72 = £27,

£4·86 × 9 = £43·74, $\frac{7}{8}$ of £40 = £35,

£26·82 ÷ 3 = £8·94, $\frac{1}{8}$ of £336 = £42,

$\frac{7}{9}$ of £27 = £21, £263·15 ÷ 5 = £52·63,

£3·93 × 6 = £23·58, $\frac{3}{4}$ of £44 = £33,

$\frac{1}{3}$ of £84 = £28, £5·22 × 6 = £31·32,

$\frac{2}{3}$ of £72 = £48, £84·60 ÷ 9 = £9·40,

$\frac{1}{7}$ of £245 = £35, $\frac{3}{5}$ of £65 = £39,

£4·62 × 7 = £32·34, $\frac{1}{5}$ of £225 = £45,

$\frac{3}{7}$ of £49 = £21, $\frac{1}{4}$ of £108 = £27,

$\frac{5}{6}$ of £42 = £35, £6·14 × 8 = £49·12,

$\frac{1}{10}$ of £460 = £46, £2·63 × 5 = £13·15,

$\frac{1}{6}$ of £336 = £56, £162·48 ÷ 4 = £40·62

Page 120

Objective
- Use a protractor to measure acute and obtuse angles to the nearest degree.

Differentiation
◔ Use an overhead projector to remind the children how to measure and draw angles to the nearest degree. Revize previous work on calculating angles at a point (see spring term, unit 8 and summer term unit 3). Check that the children can identify each of the angles for Section C.

◑ Draw a large quadrilateral and add the diagonals. Measure each of the angles in the shape to the nearest 1°.

Answers

A
1 35°
2 80°
3 73°
4 102°
5 148°

B 6-12 Answers will vary.

C
13 67°
14 85°
15 58°
16 40°
17 97°
18 111°

D
19 110°
20 62°
21 54°
22 40°

Challenge

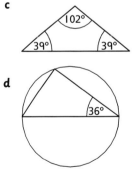

a 68° 70° 42°

b 96° 85° 54° 125°

c 102° 39° 39°

d 36°

Objective
- Solve a problem by extracting and interpreting information presented in tables, graphs and charts.

Differentiation
🌑 Work in pairs for Section B. In the *Challenge* check that children can interpret information presented in the football league table: P = played, W = win, D = draw, L = loss, F = goals for, A = goals against, GD = goal difference. In the results table: og = own goal, pen = penalty, scores in brackets are half-time scores and the names and numbers are the goal scorers and the times of the goals.
🌑 Extend the *Challenge* by working out the total points score for each team if there are 2 points for a win, 1 point for a draw and 0 points for a loss. Write five questions about the

Answers

A 1 *2: red or black*
2 4 results: red, red or red, black or black, red or black, black
3

1st card	2nd card	3rd card
R	R	R
R	R	B
R	B	R
R	B	B
B	R	R
B	R	B
B	B	R
B	B	B

4 8 results 6 32 results
5 16 results 7 1024 results

B 8 4: heart, club, diamond or spade
9 16: HH, HC, HD, HS, CH, CC, CD, CS, DH, DC, DD, DS, SH, SC, SD, SS
10 64 results 12 1024 results
11 256 results 13 1 048 576 results

Challenge
a 4 goals   c 2 penalties   e see table
b 2 own goals   d 12 goals   below

Table	P	W	D	L	F	A	GD	Pts
Barlow	9	9	0	0	29	9	20	27
Dibton	9	9	0	0	26	10	16	27
Holt	10	7	3	0	22	11	11	24
Farlow	10	6	4	0	16	8	8	22
Byfield	9	4	3	2	21	16	5	15
Pegham	10	3	1	6	14	14	0	10
Hope	10	3	1	6	12	14	⁻2	10
Pitsea	9	3	0	6	15	17	⁻2	9
Matton	9	3	0	6	6	15	⁻9	9
Keld	10	2	2	6	10	25	⁻15	8
Coombe	9	1	0	8	8	21	⁻13	3
Aston	10	0	0	10	4	23	⁻19	0

Objective
- Read and plot co-ordinates in all four quadrants.

Differentiation
🌑 Extend the work in Section A by writing the co-ordinates of four points, one in each quadrant, that when joined together in order with straight lines produce a square; a rectangle; a parallelogram. For the *Challenge*, instead of designing a golf course, draw a fence that is 200 m long, a track that is 1000 m long, etc.

Answers

A

1 kite
2 hexagon
3 trapezium
4 rectangle

Question	5		6
Tee	Tee	Flag	Length
no 1	(⁻2,1)	(⁻5,5)	500 m
no 2	(⁻6,4)	(⁻8,2)	280 m
no 3	(⁻6,2)	(⁻8,⁻4)	630 m
no 4	(⁻8,⁻5)	(⁻5,⁻4)	320 m
no 5	(⁻5,⁻3)	(⁻1,⁻4)	410 m
no 6	(⁻2,⁻3)	(4,⁻2)	610 m
no 7	(5,⁻2)	(2,⁻5)	420 m
no 8	(3,⁻5)	(7,⁻5)	570 m (dog leg)
no 9	(8,⁻5)	(6,0)	540 m
no 10	(7,0)	(8,4)	410 m
no 11	(7,5)	(1,5)	630 m (dog leg)
no 12	(0,5)	(4,3)	450 m
no 13	(5,3)	(7,4)	220 m
no 14	(7,3)	(3,⁻1)	570 m
no 15	(2,⁻2)	(⁻4,⁻2)	600 m
no 16	(⁻5,⁻2)	(⁻1,0)	450 m
no 17	(0,1)	(⁻3,4)	420 m
no 18	(⁻2,5)	(2,0)	640 m

Challenge
Answers will vary.

Page 123

Answers

A
1 42·6
2 0·345
3 2840
4 2·384
5 494
6 616·5

B
7 44·23, 42·3, 42, 4·4, 4·23
8 16·92, 16·29, 9·62, 6·92, 1·692
9 211·3, 121·3, 32·1, 21·3, 12·23
10 83·07, 8·37, 8·307, 3·87, 3·807

C
11 $\frac{3}{5}$
12 $\frac{5}{12}$
13 $\frac{3}{10}$
14 $\frac{2}{3}$
15 $\frac{6}{11}$
16 $\frac{2}{3}$

D
17 £28·80
18 £36
19 £206·08
20 £675
21 £45
22 £99·05

E
23 17 172
24 25 795
25 10 788
26 29 475
27 32 504
28 19
29 56
30 59
31 89
32 82

F
33 119°
34 61°
35 58°
36 29°
37 61°
38 61°

G
39 range 4, mode 5, median 6, mean 6
40 range 8, mode 2 and 7, median 3, mean 4
41 range 6, mode 7, median 7, mean 6
42 range 9, mode 4, median 6, mean 6

H
43 2n + 3
44 3n + 3
45 2n − 1
46 4n − 2

I
47 £3·63
48 £10·56

Page 124

Answers

A
1 8·534
2 18·728
3 44·418
4 29·115
5 5·746
6 14·335
7 8·011
8 304·602

B
9 154 m²

C
10 6 cm × 4 cm, 5 cm × 3 cm, 6 cm × 5 cm, 3 cm × 4 cm
11 81 cm²

D
12 0·9
13 8
14 1000
15 1000
16 10

E
17 37·5 kg
18 23·3 ml
19 £40
20 142 km
21 390 cl

F
22 48 cm
23 128 cm²

G
24 6888
25 12 173
26 8092
27 12 834
28 11 136
29 24 076
30 29·96
31 52·72
32 6·2
33 10·5

H
34 $2^3 \times 5$
35 2^6
36 2×3^3
37 3×5^2
38 $2^3 \times 5^2$
39 $2^6 \times 5$

I
40 £39
41 £32
42 £63
43 £95
44 £114

J
45 $\frac{5}{16}$
46 $\frac{3}{5}$
47 $\frac{1}{8}$
48 $\frac{1}{3}$
49 $\frac{3}{25}$
50 $\frac{8}{25}$

K
51 123°
52 84°
53 39°
54 63°
55 90°

Page 125

Objectives
- Solve mathematical problems or puzzles, recognize and explain patterns and relationships, generalize and predict.
- Choose and use appropriate number operations to solve problems and appropriate ways of calculating: mental, mental with jottings, written methods, calculator.
- Explain methods and reasoning.

Differentiation
- Discuss possible strategies before children start work on the padlock problem. Children work in pairs or in small groups. Use a calculator to work out or check answers.
- Write a set of rules for a partner to explain how to complete the target.

Answers

There are 676 000 possible code combinations for the padlock (26 × 10 × 10 × 10 × 26).

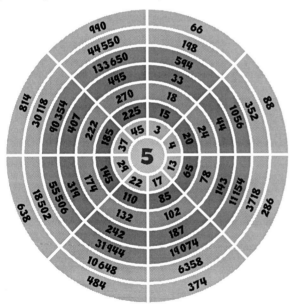

To find the numbers in each sector:

purple = red number 5 × green

brown = green + purple

blue = purple + brown

pink = brown × blue

yellow = pink ÷ 3

grey = yellow ÷ green

sum of grey = 66 + 88 + 286 + 374 + 484 + 638 + 814 + 990 = 3740

sum of green = 3 + 4 + 13 + 17 + 22 + 29 + 37 + 45 = 170

3740 ÷ 170 = 22, key 22 opens the safe

Page 126

Objectives
- Solve mathematical problems or puzzles, recognize and explain patterns and relationships, generalize and predict.
- Explain methods and reasoning.
- Choose and use appropriate number operations to solve problems and appropriate ways of calculating: mental, mental with jottings, written methods, calculator.

Differentiation
- Children work in pairs.
- Be more specific about the expectations of the game, e.g. it should last for approximately 10 minutes, it should be a game for practising multiplication tables, etc.